If God knows it all,

WHY

Do We Pray?

The Necessity of Prayer

Copyright

Title: If God knows it all, why do we pray?

Author: Goitseone Jennifer Lenyatso

1st Edition

© 2018, Goitseone Jennifer Lenyatso

Tokyo, Japan

2nd Edition

© 2019, Goitseone Jennifer Lenyatso

Gaborone, Botswana

goitsie@yahoo.com

LEN Printers & Publishers

P. O. Box 53236

Gaborone

Contact: 71907345 / 3111301

ISBN 978-1-7188-5190-0

Dedicated to ...

My Mother, Seamogano Tsie. Mama, you are my role Model, I
have learnt to trust in God because of you.
I love you.

TABLE OF CONTENTS

Preface

One Great Man of God once said, *"If there are tears in Heaven, it will be because we do not pray enough..."*

CHAPTER 1

WHAT IS PRAYER?

PRAYER is communication with God.

Prayer can be described as the primary and best way for believers in Jesus Christ to communicate their emotions, feelings and desires with God and to fellowship with Him. In other words, praying is basically talking to God; it can be making requests, petitions, worship, praise, being thankful and appealing to Him; and as long as it involves a form of communication with God, then it can be safely titled PRAYER!

Prayer time is an intimate time spent with God. We can spend time in church, we can read our Bibles and even have a pile of devotionals next to our beds, and read all Christians books we can lay our hands on, but if there is no prayer, there is automatically no communication with God, and if we do not communicate with Him, there would be a weak, or no relationship between us and Him

Just like a parent and their child spending time together, THERE IS NO substitute for one-on-one time with the Lord - Prayer!

Prayer is not only about talking to God, it's also about listening to His voice; all communication has to be both ends, not one sided.

One thing we have to note is that spending time with God reflects in every other part of our lives, especially if done on a regular basis. It is easy to recognize a prayerful Christian; the Christian who spends quality time communicating with God, simply because prayer strengthens the relationship of the Christian and God.

The way such Christian speaks, relates with others and conducts themselves always reflects somehow.

It is perhaps very important for us to spend that one-on-one time with God through prayer because no one knows us like God, He is our Creator and He keeps all of our secrets. He is the best person to confide in, to share our fears and secrets with, without fear of being judged, laughed at or dismissed.

The other important thing to note is that prayer should not be mistaken for meditation. While the fundamental aspect of meditation is keeping quiet and doing it on certain times and certain places, prayer is direct access and address to God, which can be done anytime, anywhere and anyhow, including speaking, crying or even groaning.

Prayer also has its own rules; *all prayer must be offered in faith (James 1:6), in the name of the Lord Jesus (John 16:23), and in the power of the Holy Spirit (Romans 8:26)*

In short, a Christian prayer is addressed to God as the Heavenly Father, in the name of Jesus Christ as the Mediator, and through the enabling grace of the indwelling Holy Spirit. When the disciples of Jesus

Christ asked Him how they should pray, He started with *'Our Father who art in heaven..'*

This clearly shows that prayer is supposed to be offered to the Heavenly Father, our God and Him alone!

It should be however be noted that the wicked have no desire to pray *(Psalm 10:4),* but the children of God have a natural desire to pray *(Luke 11:1)* just like communication between a child and their parent comes effortlessly and naturally.

Like stated above, prayer can be done anyhow, meaning that it can be audible, silent, private, public, formal, informal in any posture one feels compelled to do it in. Some people love praying on their knees, others walking around, others driving, others lying down. Also is there nowhere in the bible where it is stated how one should dress while in prayer, putting on pants, dresses, skirts, is permissible....perhaps half naked or stark naked is also acceptable...???

As much as people care more about the outward appearance, God cares more about the heart. I once said to my friends, if it was not for Eve and Adam to eat that fruit in the garden of Eden, maybe we would be living together, without any clothes....remember they realized their nakedness only after eating the fruit...

Anyway, that's a topic for another day; now continuing on prayer, Paul wrote, *"Do not be anxious about anything, but in every situation, by prayer and petition, with thanksgiving, present your requests to God.*

And the peace of God, which transcends all understanding, will guard your hearts and your minds in Christ Jesus" (Philippians 4:6-7).

In essence, this means that in any situation, worry about nothing; but pray about everything, and while at it, give thanks. To be honest, where there is prayer, there is little to no room for worry and anxiety.

Try it one day and take some time in prayer when you are stressed, you will suddenly feel peace and calmness engulfing you - the wonderful works of prayer!

One thing to highlight regarding prayer again is that God wants us to talk with Him about everything. He is always ready to listen to us.

Isaiah 59:1 'Surely the arm of the LORD is not too short to save, nor his ear too dull to hear.'

Not only always ready to listen but also to answer us. *Isn't it that Matthew 7:7 says ask and it shall be given to you...?*

You see how we are missing out by praying less?

There is so much we can gain, only if we pray.

There are many reasons we take time to converse with our heavenly father through prayer, it can be to praise God, to thank Him, to tell Him how we feel about Him, including how much we love Him. Telling God that you love Him is praying, telling Him that He is great, that you thank Him, is PRAYING!

We pray to enjoy His presence; if He is too far from us, communication with Him would maybe need a cell phone or a pen and paper to write a letter to Him. But because He is an omnipresent God, we pray knowing that He is with us, and being in His presence is beautiful.

We pray to make our requests and seek guidance and ask for wisdom from God. Asking God for something shows how dependent we are on Him, it also shows how much faith and trust we have on Him, if we didn't believe that He can answer us, we obviously wouldn't take time to pray.

One way to look at prayer is from a relationship point, like I have mentioned in some instances above, as parents, we constantly talk to our children, and we love it, communication is what keeps our relationship with our children, or everyone around us strong and going, similarly, God loves talking with His children - us; our communication with Him, keeps our relationship with Him going.

Fellowship with God is the heart of prayer.

Too often we lose sight of how essential prayer really is. We get caught in thinking prayer is one of the things we can only do when we have trouble, but that is not true. We have been advised to pray without ceasing, this means we out to pray and not lose heart, we ought to pray, in sickness and in health, in and ought of season, in wealth or poverty, happy or unhappy, when things are all fine and when everything has fallen apart.......

May God give us the Grace to pray as much when everything is going great in our lives, as we pray when things are not great in our lives in Jesus Mighty Name!!

Further on reasons for praying, through our prayers, we admit that God is greater than us and ultimately knows what is best in any given situation *(Romans 11:33-36).*

Just that act of praying, is a reflection of humility to God, acceptance of who He is, an exercise of faith as we would be believing that He can change the situation. Non-verbally, praying is a way of telling God that we trust Him that much.

Again, through prayer, we essentially say, "Not my will, but Your will"; it is being selfless and open to the purpose of our maker for us.

Most importantly, everyone expects a response through an answered prayer after praying; but to get that answer is in the hands of God, our role is to pray according to the will of God and in accordance with His Word.

Quoting scriptures when praying is not an option but compulsory, reminding God of His words and promises will always get His attention, and this comes naturally even between us human beings.

Prayer is not self-seeking, not our will, but seeking to align ourselves with the will of God more and more *(1 John 5:14; James 4:3).*

Many people live frustrated and confused lives, because their motive for asking or making requests to God, is wrong, in other words, they pray amiss! It is important to note that our motive for asking God for anything matters. If you ask for a blessing of a car because someone has bought a new car and you want to keep up, it's highly unlikely that God will give it to you..

There are no special formulas/methods of praying, neither is there a particular time, day or way of praying e.g. sitting, kneeling, standing etc., in fact you can be walking and praying to God as you would be talking with your friend. You could be driving and praying to God, you could be showering and praying to God.

Praying is just like talking to your father, mother or close friend, and this is something that should not be hard to do, just like it is not hard to talk to my friend or parent.

My believe is that it is very easy to talk to God, yet so many of us seem not to be able to find a few minutes each day to talk to our Heavenly Father,

Creator, Deliverer and Sustainer. You would be surprised at what a fifteen-minute prayer offered in the morning can achieve....

Many people only talk to God when life is tough, but if doing this, finding time to pray when we need help with something, are in trouble or need money or just need something from God like it currently is, would we like it if our children talked to us only when they wanted something from us or were in some kind of trouble?

Definitely NO!!

The fact is, talking is one important way in which we as humans build relationships because we are social beings.

Just like how we talk to others to maintain relationships, our Heavenly Father expects the same from us, He even begs us to talk to Him.

Simply because He created us to have a close relationship with Him.

God used to visit Adam and Eve in the Garden of Eden to just talk, about any and everything *(Genesis 3:8-9).* And this has not changed; God wants to hear from His creation even today.

CHAPTER 2

IF GOD KNOWS IT ALL, WHY DO WE PRAY?

GOD IS ALL-POWERFUL, all-knowing and loving.

Jesus urged His disciples to trust God as a loving Father, and taught them to pray, asking God for daily sustenance, forgiveness and the ability to forgive others, and even for our daily food; this we agree..

But if God already knows what we need and is in charge, why do we need to pray at all?

It's sometimes easy to fall into the trap of thinking, God knows my every thought and all my needs. It's easy and common to ask ourselves questions;

He loves me and has promised to care for me. So why do I need to pray?

If God does not change and is eternal and knows the beginning and the end, then why should I ask for something He might not be willing to give me?

Or why would I tell Him about things He already knows?

Why should I tell Him of my cares, if I trust He is good and cares for me?

These are reasonable and understandable questions.

They exhibit an understanding of the sovereignty of God over all creation and His goodness and kindness, His mercy and love, as well as the gifts of abundant grace that He gives us every day.

But still, we have to pray.

Prayer is so significant that, in the book of *Luke 11:1*, after Jesus spent ample time with His disciples, them witnessing the miracles, deliverances, healing and resurrections He carried out, still they asked Him to teach them how to pray... question is, didn't they know how to pray? They definitely knew, but they realized the significance of prayer!

The disciples of Jesus Christ did not ask Him to teach them how to prophesy, how to preach or teach, how to perform signs and wonders, how to heal the sick or how to read the bible, but they asked about prayer, because they knew that through it, then they will manage to do all these things!

REASONS TO PRAY TO GOD THOUGH HE KNOWS IT ALL

1. Connection

AS HUMAN BEINGS, we have been created by God, and if we do not connect with Him, there is that gap that we feel which only Him can occupy. We pray because of this natural connection we have with our Creator. Just like the natural connection we have with our children as their parents.

Naturally, we want to be close to people who loves us, and this includes God, who made us, someone who we are very sure that He cares about us, therefore we pray to sustain and deepen our relationship with Him.

Conversation through prayer is a necessary part of this connection. Submitting ourselves to God in prayer changes us, and fills that gap.

Every time we pray, we connect with Him more and more, in a way a human mind cannot explain nor comprehend.

2. **We are commanded and invited to Pray**

(i) PRAYER as a command.

We are expected to keep all the commands of the Lord, failure of which is disobedience, and we know that obedience is better than sacrifice!

Following commands comes with benefits, we are promised to be made the heads not tails, to be always at the top and not at the bottom, simply by observing and following the commands of the Most High. *Deuteronomy 28:13*

One thing we have to know about commands is that it is equivalent to an order! In the army when a command comes, no one asks questions, they simply follow the command, and such is the word of God when it comes to prayer! Pray and stop asking questions, just like a soldier taking an order from their commander! Just do it!

Failure to follow the commands of God is costly, it can even make you lose your son-ship, just like failure to take commands in the army can lead to one getting fired!

To mention but a few:

Matthew 5:44 'pray for them which despitefully use you, and persecute you...'

Mark 13:33 'Take heed, watch and pray..'

Luke 18: 1 'And he spoke a parable unto them to this end, that men ought always to pray, and not to faint..'

Ephesians 6:18 'Praying always with all prayer and supplication in the Spirit...'

Romans 12:12 'Rejoicing in hope; patient in tribulation; continuing instant in prayer..'

Colossians 4:2 'Continue in prayer..'

1 Thessalonians 5:17 'Pray without ceasing..'

My friend, we have been commanded to pray.

Praying is for our benefit, not for the benefit of God.

He is the same yesterday, today and forever, if you choose not to pray to Him, He still is God and loses nothing! - but you stand to lose if you don't pray, He doesn't lose if you don't pray.

(ii) PRAYER as an Invitation

Psalm 50:15 'And call upon me in the day of trouble...'

Jeremiah 29:12 'Then shall ye call upon me, and ye shall go and pray unto me...'

Matthew 7:7-11 'Ask, and it shall be given you; seek, and ye shall find; knock, and it shall be opened unto you..'

We are invited to pray because God loves us and desires to have a relationship with us and we are to respond to these.

When He calls us to something we are to respond as the Prophet Isaiah did, *"here am I." (Isaiah 6:8)*

Responding to God in prayer is not only an act of obedience, it is also an act of honor given to the One who gave His all for us; the One who calls us to pray.

31

Furthermore, obedience is better than sacrifice. It is better to pray than not to.

3. **Jesus Prayed**

"AFTER HE HAD dismissed them, He went up on a mountainside by Himself to pray." Matthew 14:23

"Then Jesus went with his disciples to a place called Gethsemane, and He said to them, 'Sit here while I go over there and pray.'" –Matthew 26:36

"Very early in the morning, while it was still dark, Jesus got up, left the house and went off to a solitary place, where he prayed." –Mark 1:35

"But Jesus often withdrew to lonely places and prayed." –Luke 5:16

"One of those days Jesus went out to a mountainside to pray and spent the night praying to God." –Luke 6:12

"Then Jesus told his disciples a parable to show them that they should always pray and not give up." –Luke 18:1

Jesus Christ is our role model. We are to follow in His footsteps, if He saw it necessary to pray, we should do the same.

We are told to be conformed to the image of Jesus (Romans 8:29). Prayer was a regular part of the Lord's daily life and it has to be part of ours also.

Although He was and it still God, Jesus prayed because He was living in a human body just like us now.

When Jesus set aside His divinity *(Philippians 2:7)*, He no longer shared the union with God that He had in glory, hence to Jesus, prayer was just as it is for us now - a personal way of communicating with God.

Be motivated to be like Him.

4. Prayer is a tool we can use for our advantage

IF A PARENT makes a tool and tells their child that whenever they need help, in anything, they can use it, wouldn't it be weird if a child does not use it, even when they need help?

If you are that parent, how will you feel if the child does not use the tool?

Such is prayer, it is a tool we have been given by our Father in Heaven to use, to our advantage.

The choice to use it is ours.

At the end, reality is that prayer changes everything, situations and even lives.

People have been healed because someone offered prayer for them, some have been set free of demonic captivity because of prayer, others got employed because of prayer.

And all these wouldn't have happened, if there was no prayer!

Its upon you to pray...

Jesus said we should ask and our powerful God will answer (Luke 18:1-8).

James said we don't receive from God because we don't ask (James 4:2-3).

Matthew 7:9-11 or Luke 11:11-12. If we ask God for a fish, He will not give us a snake.

God wants to bless us and give us what we ask for, the condition is, He will give it to us, when we ask. An answer comes after something was done, or said. If we are going to expect a lot from God without prayer, then we are deceiving ourselves.

Nevertheless, God could give us what we want even if we do not ask, but if we ask and He gives it to us, it helps us to be closer to Him because we realize that God loves us, He is faithful by answering our prayers.

Asking for something and getting it, is a good thing. It increases our confidence, love and faith in God.

There is a lot that God has in store for us, but He is waiting for us to just ask. How hard can asking be??

Looking at the Parable of the Persistent Widow in *Luke 18:1-8*

"Then Jesus told his disciples a parable to show them that they should always pray and not give up. He said: "In a certain town there was a judge who neither feared God nor cared what people thought. And there was a widow in that town who kept coming to him with the plea, 'Grant me justice against my adversary.'

"For some time he refused. But finally he said to himself, 'Even though I don't fear God or care what people think, yet because this widow keeps bothering me, I will see that she gets justice, so that she won't eventually come and attack me!'"

And the Lord said, "Listen to what the unjust judge says. And will not God bring about justice for his chosen ones, who cry out to him day and night? Will he keep putting them off? I tell you, he will see that they get justice, and quickly. However, when the Son of Man comes, will he find faith on the earth?"

In this passage, we are assured that if we continually ask, we will receive what we ask for.

Persistence is key to receiving what we ask for, nothing is hard for God to do, but sometimes we have to show Him that we seriously want that which we request from Him by not giving up and being persistent.

Asking is a very important doorway to receiving.

But just like a parent to a child, we should note that God is not forced to agree to every request we make before Him.

He can say either yes or no.

I know this because I am a parent. If my child demands something, I sometimes do the same.

The answer is not always yes.

If I raise my kids to always agree to them, it will backfire to me later on in life; as a parent I should know better.

There are things my kids would ask from me which I would know that is if by any chance give it to them, they may hurt themselves, and likewise, such is God. He keeps certain things from us sometimes for our own good.

And as much as we still love our kids when we refuse to give them everything, God loves us even when He says no.

Again, as much as our children can never manipulate us to give them what they want, we also cannot manipulate God to give us what we want from Him-He would know the intends of our hearts before we even try to do.

There are no laws about prayer, but there are general principles applicable when praying. Some of the principles are as below:

God will give us what we ask for in **humility** *(John 14:13-14, Matthew 7:9-11)*;

We need to keep on asking **persistently** *(Luke 18:1-8)*.

In addition, if we ask for something that is outside **His will** (like asking for permission to sin), then the answer will be no *(1 John 5:14-15)*, and if we ask out of purely selfish **motives**, the answer will also be no *(James 4:3)*.

While praying, it is important to remember that prayer is not principally about asking God for things, of course we can use prayer to receive from God, but we should not forget that prayer is more importantly about expressing our love to God, our worship, praise of Him and pouring out our hearts and desires to Him.

5. **Prayer Changes things**

SOME THINGS HAVE happened only because they were prayed for; meaning that they would not have happened if they were not prayed for. Although we must never presume God will grant us apart from prayer what He has ordained to grant us only by means of prayer, God responds to prayer.

Moses prayed for food and water for the Israelites *(Exodus 15 and Numbers 11),* and they were given to him.

Hannah prayed for a child *(1 Samuel 1)* and she indeed had her child.

Elijah prayed for drought and then rain *(1 Kings 18–19).*

The events took place because someone took time to pray for them.

Although God had already determined them, they still had to be prayed for, for them to came to pass. They would not have taken place if these men and women of God did not pray for them.

To say we don't need to pray because God has determined all outcomes is as ridiculous as saying we don't need to take medicine, work for a living, or look for a spouse because God has determined all outcomes.

It is true God has determined all outcomes, but God has also determined the means by which those outcomes will take place.

And one of those is to pray first.

If God has determined that a barren woman will have a child one day, then He has also determined the prayers on her behalf, not to mention the birth of the gynaecologist and other medical specialists who would treat her and the opening of a medical school in those specialists would have studied at.

Prayers are one of the many means God uses to unlock what He has determined. Such that sometimes if we do not pray, what He has determined does not come to pass.

Similarly, if God has determined that someone will decide to follow Christ in 2020, then He has also determined the births of the people who will share the gospel with her and the prayers offered on her behalf.

The above has already been decided, therefore one of the things that really cause it to happen, may be the very prayer that we are now offering daily in our churches for more and more people to give their lives to Christ across the globe.

Your prayer contributes to what God has determined. Hence a need to continue praying!

Again, God determines both the ends and the means, including the prayers we offer. We do not know what we ought to pray for, but through the help of the Holy Spirit, we do pray.

In essence, God gives us the privilege of including us in His work if we are willing and allowing Him.

If your understanding of God leads you to pray less, then you need to rethink your understanding of who God is.

There are events that will not happen, souls that will not be saved, and relationships that will not be restored unless we pray for them.

Our prayers make things happen.

This insight alone should bring us to our knees.

6. Prayer is valuable to God

PRAYER ITSELF IS valuable to God. Two wonderful demonstrations of this are found in *Hebrews 7:25 and Revelation 5:8*. In the first passage the writer informs us of the occupation and passion of the Lord Jesus since His ascension: "...Since He always lives to make intercession for them."

Think of it: "He always lives to make Intercession." Prayer, then, is so important to the Lord that it has been perhaps one of the main roles of Christ since He left earth. God obviously values it in a way we usually do not.

In *Revelation 5*, we are admitted to a rare view of heaven's throne room. We do not have many illustrative descriptions of heaven, but this is one of the most vivid. In it, we see the four living creatures, the twenty-four elders, the Lamb (Christ), and God the Father.

The book of the Judgement of God is being given to the Lamb, and the verse reads: *"And when He had taken the book, the four living creatures and the* *twenty-four elders fell down before the Lamb, having each one a harp, and golden bowls full of incense which are the **prayers** of the saints"*

In heaven, prayer is seen as incense. Interestingly, incense is used for fragrance, and that is the beauty of perfume.

Consider that there were other choices He could have made to be incense in heaven.

But He chose the prayers of the saints!

This is how important our prayers are. Without them, there would be no incense in Heaven.

Imagine that He could have used service, or Bible Study, or witnessing, or hard work, or tithing, or church attendance, or any one of a number of wonderful Christian activities as incense. Yet, in His perfect wisdom He chose prayer.

Another perfect example of how God values prayer can be found in the book *of Mark 11:17, "Then He taught, saying to them, 'Is it not written, "My house shall be called a house of prayer for all nations"? But you have made it a den of thieves.'*

In the above scripture, Jesus was angry when He found people trading and selling things in a church. He specifically *said His house is a house of prayer!!!*

He could have said it's a house of worship, a house of praise, a house of joy, a house of peace, a house of preaching, but He said a house of PRAYER!

This is how God sees the church and prayer – the two are inseparable; prayer should be central in any church of Christ; prayer is more important than anything we can ever do in church!

When we enter heaven for the first time and fall on our faces before Him, the aroma we will notice will be that of intercession.

All of which makes us ask:

"How long do we usually take praying in our churches?"

"Do we see church like Jesus saw it?"

"If God values prayer that much, how much do we value it?"

Certainly, prayer has to be the center of our Christian and spiritual walk.

7. There is Power in Prayer

John 14:13-14 – 'And whatsoever ye shall ask in my name, that will I do, that the Father may be glorified in the Son.'

1 John 5:14-15– 'And this is the confidence that we have in him, that, if we ask any thing according to his will, he hears us..'

James 1:5– 'If any of you lack wisdom, let him ask of God, that giveth to all [men] liberally, and upbraideth not; and it shall be given him'.

James 5:16 ...'The effectual fervent prayer of a righteous man availeth much.'

Luke 11:9– 'And I say unto you, Ask, and it shall be given you; seek, and ye shall find; knock, and it shall be opened unto you.'

The power in prayer is not a power that comes from the act of prayer. It is a power that flows from the One to whom we pray to.

In His Omnipotence He responds and we receive—

that's the power of prayer!

Prayer unleashes a deeper communion with God in our hearts and it comforts our souls.

It grows a richer faith in who He is and unleashes power in us to live our lives in service to Him and others.

The power is not in our petition. The power comes from His response.

Prayer is so powerful that if done on a regular basis, it changes character and conduct, a once violent aggressive arrogant person would suddenly become so soft and humble. And such is prayer!

A person who was under captivity of drinking alcohol, doing drugs, being addicted to anything, is able to be set free, only where prayers are being offered!

Childhood scars and grudges are able to be forgotten, only after prayer! There is healing, reconciliations, deliverance, where prayer is!

CHAPTER 3

THE POWER OF PRAYER

❖ **Peace**

AFTER ME AND my husband lost our son, we were overwhelmed with this kind of peace that we could not understand.

It did not make sense to us and to people around us. It took us time to understand that the peace we have is because of our constant stand in prayer. The word of God was alive in our lives.

Peace is perhaps the most desired emotional gift God can give someone in tough situations.

The fact is, when we take all your troubles to someone we believe can handle them better, its relieving of the burdens and stresses associated with having to carry such loads for ourselves.

Why not casting all your cares upon God because He cares for you? *(1 Peter 5:7)*

He bids us, *"Come to Me, all you who labor and are heavy laden, and I will give you rest." (Matthew 11:28)*

And has promised, *"Peace I leave with you, My peace I give to you; not as the world gives do I give to you. Let not your heart be troubled, neither let it be afraid." (John 14:27)*

Be anxious for nothing, but in everything by prayer and supplication, with thanksgiving, let your requests be made known to God; and the peace of God, which surpasses all understanding, will guard your hearts and minds through Christ Jesus. (Philippians 4:6, 7)

Colossians 3:15 says, "And let the peace of Christ arbitrate in your hearts, to which also you were called in one Body, and be thankful."

This kind of peace isn't just freedom from worry, but the peace in our hearts, which can transform to peace between different people, which can end in peace between nations; if prayer was made the center in every individual on earth.

How can we, as believers, let the peace of Christ arbitrate in all our relationships with people, especially other believers that are different from us? **It's only by our prayer.**

When we pray, Christ will become the real ultimate, ruler, and decider in everything we do.

Such prayer preserves the peace in our marriage life, family life, Christian life and church life. This arbitrating peace is a great benefit of prayer!

Also, a number of scientific studies have shown that regular prayer is an important factor in living longer and staying healthy.

"It doesn't matter if you pray for yourself or for others, pray to heal an illness or for peace in the world, or simply sit in silence and quiet the mind—the effects appear to be the same.

Jesus called the weak and weary to come to Him for rest.

Come to Me, all you who labor and are heavily burdened, and I will give you rest. Take My yoke upon you, and learn from Me. For I am meek and lowly in heart, and you will find rest for your souls. For My yoke is easy, and My burden is light." Matthew 11:28

When one feels weak and cannot do anything anymore, calling onto Jesus can rescue them, when one is tired of this life, calling onto Jesus will give them hope.

In the book of Jeremiah, when Prophet Jeremiah felt overwhelmed by his task, he turned to the Lord for renewal. It was through prayer that the prophet lamented, grieved, and found strength to continue his ministry.

Likewise, prayer is an avenue by which we may share our heart to God and fully process everything that weighs down our spirit.

When we are down in the dumps, prayer gives us hope.

This world is filled with stress. We are constantly bombarded with responsibilities, challenges, and pressures. Daily troubles and stress will surround us as long as we live in this world.

But when we lay our troubles at God's feet in prayer, we can feel the weight of the world tumbling off of our shoulders. God's peace fills us as we know He hears our prayers.

God can calm the storm in your life even when you are in the middle of it. Like Peter, we have to keep our eyes on Jesus to stop from sinking under the weight of our problems. But when we do this, we can walk on water.

Each new day, turn your pressures over to God in prayer and feel your stress levels go down.

❖ Healing can come through prayer

SECOND TO HAVING peace of mind after losing our son, God healed us. The pain of losing a child is comparable to nothing. We needed to be healed, in all aspects, physically, mentally, emotionally and even spiritually.

And through prayer, the healing came, rather quickly. We were able to put the past behind us and focus on the future. Even the pain we felt lessened as we prayed more.

None can offer true healing in all dimensions of the whole person like God did for us; He indeed is the Greatest Physician.

Besides this that He did for us, God is willing to do the same or even more for anyone, when one is sick, by calling upon the name of the Lord, they can be healed. The bible says by the stripes of Jesus Christ, we are healed.

God's desire is for us to be in good health, if our health fails us, we can go to Him and He can heal and restore us.

"For I will restore health to you and heal you of your wounds. (1 John 2)

"If you diligently heed the voice of the Lord your God and do what is right in His sight, give ear to His commandments and keep all His statutes, I will put none of the diseases on you which I have brought on the Egyptians. For I am the Lord who heals you." (Exodus 15:26)

In *Isaiah 38*, King Hezekiah prayed for healing and he was healed.

God is waiting for you to get your healing, don't delay, Pray!

Prayer also has been proven to help regulate human heartbeat, making it stronger and less stressed. Personally, when I have heart palpitations and start praying, they subside, the heartbeat slows down and becomes normal. And this is one of the tangible benefits of prayer I have experienced.

Though it is a mental and spiritual activity, prayer also has been known to speed up the recovery of the heart following heart attacks and cardiac surgery.

By minimizing all the life-threatening effects of stress and environmental factors, praying helps our bodies to heal more efficiently and age more smoothly.

Regarding recovery, after a situation leaves you emotionally or physically distraught, there is need for recovery and this is a timely process.

And prayer can serve as a way to deal with the aftermath of such and help keep our faith. As our minds and bodies are focused solely on healing, prayer will keep us centered, hopeful and sometimes sane.

Acts 28:8-9 Publius' father was sick in bed, suffering from fever and dysentery. Paul went in to see him and, after prayer, placed his hands on him and healed him.

Acts 9:40 "Peter sent them all out of the room; then he got down on his knees and prayed.

Turning toward the dead woman, he said, "Tabitha, get up." She opened her eyes and seeing Peter she sat.

Both Paul and Peter used the same method for healing which is Prayer. Prayer can even be used to give life.

Even today, this power still stands.

❖ Prayer helps us forgive easily

WHEN WE PRAY, we open ourselves up to forgiveness. Prayer not only helps us to be forgiven but enables us to forgive others; something which is impossible without God.

After the burial of our dear son, people expected us to report the nanny to the police and have her prosecuted for neglecting our child, the very thing that lead to his death.

But we did not, we found it in our hearts to forgive her, to us, if taking her to the police would bring back the boy, then we would pursue that path, but since it wouldn't, we felt it was not worth it, but we released her from her hearts, without any bitterness nor anger. Simply because of prayer.

The fact is, there are no perfect people in this world, even Christians.

We all strive to be the best Christians we can be, but occasionally we still slip up and do wrong because of human nature.

When we fail, it is comforting to know that we can go to God in prayer to ask for forgiveness.

It is also relieving to know that we can be forgiven by those around us when we wrong them.

Also, through prayer, God can help us forgive ourselves. Sometimes we struggle with letting ourselves off the hook, yet God has already forgiven our sins.

We tend to beat ourselves up too much. But through prayer, God can help us walk free of guilt and shame and begin to like ourselves again.

If we do not pray, we will fail to forgive, and when we do not forgive, we are the ones who suffer from bitterness, resentment, and depression. Also if we do not forgive, how do we expect God to forgive us? "

"For if you forgive other people when they sin against you, your heavenly Father will also forgive you. But if you do not forgive others their sins, your Father will not forgive your sins." (Matthew 6:14-15)

Praying also helps us forgive God. When faced with tough situations, sometimes it becomes so painful that we start pointing fingers at God, accusing Him and blaming Him for what we go through. Some people can even backslide after facing certain trials because of anger and bitterness towards God, which can be understandable.

But through prayer, we can let go, and believe that everything works together for our own good.

Basically, for our own benefit and for the benefit of the person who hurt us, we must forgive.

Some people say lack of forgiveness is like drinking poison thinking that it will kill another person.

May God give us a forgiving heart in the Mighty Name of Jesus Christ!

❖ **Prayer helps us be Wise**

THERE IS WISDOM in praying.

A prayerful person is a wise person, and a wise person prays.

How different would your life be if you knew and believe that through prayer, you can tap into divine knowledge to aid you every area of life?

The Men and Women of God today whom we all look up to, admire and see as our role models because of their level of wisdom and how they can teach the word of God, spend hours and hours in prayer. If these are because of prayer, they we can be, if we pray like them..

Even those in the olden days knew this well and it was the master secret to their success, wealth, and victories.

This is evident by the kings of Israel when they sought God's counsel whether or not to go into battle or how to defeat their enemies.

There is no need to go through life confused about anything when God has promised that prayer is there to use to your advantage.

'Call to Me, and I will answer you, and show you great and mighty things, which you do not know.' (Jeremiah 33:3)

Abraham's servant prayed for divine guidance and success in his quest. (Genesis 24:12-15)

Daniel got divine wisdom and understanding to interpret King Nebuchadnezzar's dream. (Daniel 2:17-23)

King Solomon prayed for divine wisdom to lead his nation. (1 Kings 3; 2 Chronicles 1)

True wisdom, knowledge, understanding, and happiness come from God. (Proverbs 2:5-7; Ecclesiastes 2:26)

When we are in continuous prayer with God, we receive a perpetual flow of wisdom and guidance.

"If any of you lacks wisdom, let him ask of God, who gives to all liberally and without reproach, and it will be given to him." James 1:5

❖ **Prayer strengthens our faith and trust in God**

THIS SHOULD GO without saying, when you pray consistently, you develop a bond that grows with the One to Whom your prayers are directed to. You become more confident about living life to the full.

As you pray, and ask God for different needs, the more He gives you what you want, the more your faith grows, the more confident you become and the more you trust Him.

And the deeper that faith becomes, the more effective your prayers will be because, *"without faith, it is impossible to please Him, for he who comes to God must believe that He is, and that He is a rewarder of those who diligently seek Him." (Hebrews 11:6)*

'All things, whatever you ask for in prayer, believe (have faith) and you will receive them.' (Matthew 21:22)

Also, because prayer is our communion with God, each time we approach the Lord through prayer, our faith strengthens.

God promises that He hears the prayers of His people (1 John 5:14).

Again, as we see God answer our prayers with both positive and negative responses, our faith matures because we realize He is actively present in our lives.

❖ **Access to heaven's abundant resources**

ASK AND IT shall be given to you. .

When I was pregnant with my first born, I had complications and saw God come through for me. During my second pregnancy, my gynecologist was very cautious, to his surprise, throughout the pregnancy and the birth, everything went smoothly. Puzzled, he asked me if I am a prayerful person.

I said 'yes'. To him as a medical person, the challenges I had in the first pregnancy were supposed to resurface in the second one.

But they did not, because of prayer. My doctor knew this very well, that it can only be, where there is prayer!

All credit to God through my never-ending prayers, I made bold declarations about my health while expecting, and God being faithful, granted me my desires. Which ended up in something that did not make sense medically.

Why should the sons and daughters of God be reluctant to pray, when prayer is the key in the hand of faith to unlock heaven's storehouse, where there are treasured boundless resources of Omnipotence?

Prayer is an absolute for successful living.

You can't reach any worthwhile pinnacle without it. *And the One to whom you pray is able to do exceeding abundantly above all that you can ask or even think. (Ephesians 3:20)*

When I was expecting my third born, I prayed to God against pain while giving birth. Because of the strain, pressures and excitement associated with delivery, I completely forgot about my prayers.

After the delivery, I was puzzled and asked myself, 'why is it that I do not feel pain like I did in the previous births?'

I asked my gynecologist to explain to me, I was wondering if he had used a different kind of painkiller this time around, he laughed at me and said in passing, 'maybe you prayed against pain'

I was left with a dropped jaw, 'how could I forget?' Sometimes we pray and forget, but God doesn't forget. See how faithful God is?

Even when we forget our petitions to Him, He remembers!

There was a time when my husband was unemployed, I was not worried, but I was not praying for his employment, after about three months still nothing, not even an interview, I decided to pray for his employment.

I remember I started praying specifically for this on the 21st March 2018, with a three day fast, followed by daily midnight prayers. In May, he told me that he had been called for an interview in one of the mining companies.

I continued praying for him. But after the interview, there was no response, for about two full weeks!

I was not anxious, for I trusted God. When I had completely forgot about it, but still praying for his employment, he showed me an offer letter they had sent him through email.

I shook my head! How faithful is this God? Some people even right now still believe he got the job through connections, because it is not easy to get a job in a mining company and there is high unemployment. But what is impossible for God?

Absolutely Nothing!!

And see, another thing, if there were no persistent prayers for him, would he have gotten the job? I doubt...many people give up early, be confident and tell God that if I grow old asking for this I will do it! Imitate that persistent neighbor in the book of *Luke*

11:5-8 who would not give his neighbor rest until he gave him bread!

Be like that to God and see what He will do!

Remember I started praying for the same thing in March, and the answer came two months later!

Never give up in prayer no matter how long it takes with no answer!!

❖ Blessings and Miracles

AFTER GIVING BIRTH to my third born, her pediatrician told me that she has a heart murmur (her heart did not complete development and had a hole in it).

I was devastated, shocked and confused.

I asked the doctor if there can be any medicine to give her to complete the development of the heart, she said unfortunately there is none.

I told myself that I know the greatest Physician, I determined it in my heart to get into prayer for my daughter.

And without doubt, I was positive that God is going to heal her. I prayed for her in the morning, midday and evening every day without fail.

My daughter's doctor had asked me to bring the child after 2 weeks for check-up.

When we did, she ran some tests to check the heart, and unfortunately, it was still showing signs of developmental defects. Despite the fact that I had been praying and I was still praying for God to come through for her.

I had mixed feelings, I was not shaken, I had hope, I refused to give up in prayer.

The doctor told me to come again at 6 weeks, I honestly do not know what she was hoping for.

By this time, although I was in constant prayer, I had not told my husband a thing about the situation at hand.

I simply did not want to worry him, because I trusted that God will do something before he knew. I even told myself that I will share with him everything after the healing by God.

And I continued praying and trusting God for a miracle.

At 6 weeks, we met the doctor, and she again did test, painfully, disappointingly, the heart was still the same. It was like I had been living in denial and now reality was displaying itself before me.

Worried, hurt, confused, the doctor comforted me and said I should not worry, many people live well with this condition.

The doctor asked me to come for check-up after four months, as that is when scans will be carried out for further investigations to determine how bad the murmur is and to see if she will need a surgery.

I refused to accept this defect on my baby. After this, I sat my husband down and decided to break the news to him. He was hurt but wanted to be strong for me.

It was our first time to hear of this kind of defect, and now to hear of it on our child was even more devastating.

I remember in one of the follow up checkups with the doctor, I asked her for medication that will correct the defect, and she told me that there is none at all.

Nevertheless, me and my husband decided to continue to pray for our little girl, hoping and believing God for a miracle.

At four months I took my daughter to the doctor, I was not nervous, I was not worried, I don't know what I was feeling. But deep inside I had hope.

The doctor checked my daughter's heart and whispered to me '***your daughter's heart is fine***'

She was in shock, and the way she said it, it was like she had no confidence in what she is seeing and saying.

I looked at her and asked her coldly what she was saying.

She said with a big smile on her face, 'your daughter is fine...!!'

I was in shock.

I have been praying for this miracle, and now it is here and it's like a dream.

Again, I asked, 'what?!', the doctor repeated, 'she is fine'...

The condition for a miracle is difficulty, however, the condition for a great miracle is not difficulty, but impossibility.

Believe God for any miracle and He will do it! Pray big, bold prayers for blessings and miracles in your life, ministry, and business by mastering the science of effective prayers.

I claimed this miracle for my child, and so can you. When it comes to praying, never settle for less!

❖ **Prayer enables us to set our minds on the things above**

Colossians 3:2 "Set your mind on the things which are above, not on the things which are on the earth."

Trust me, there is no other way to fulfill this word except by prayer.

Prayer is the way to have our mind set on the things above. That is because proper prayer elevates our mind from our earthly concerns to God's heavenly interests.

The more time we spend with God and focus on Him by prayer, the more it will translate into our daily lives.

In a world that advocates everything that is against God, as believers, we can use prayer to remind us of all God has done for us in the past and all God has promised to do for us into the future.

❖ Prayer enables Christ to carry out His plan

PRAYER GUIDES us to the will and plan of God about our lives.

I always use prayer when I want to know God's will. I pray about my choices, and when I have 'peace' about one of the options, then I go with it."

One day I wanted to quit my job and focus on raising my kids, I had agreed with my husband, informed my loved ones about this critical decision and my employers.

But before I could write the designation letter, I decided to pray for this decision.

To my surprise, I had no peace about it.

After persistent prayer, there was a persistent lack of peace in my heart about this decision. I then decided to abort the decision.

I never explained to anyone why I changed my mind, not even my husband, but I did because God was against it.

Now when I look back, I shudder to think of where I would be, where my family would be, had I left my job.

Through prayer, God guided me to His will and plan, am grateful. If I did not pray about this, I would have made the biggest mistake of my life!

And even today, many people get into bad marriages, because of prayerlessness; many take decisions they live to regret, because of failure to pray...

May God give us the grace to consult Him first in every decision we make in Jesus Mighty Name!

When we do this, Jesus will guide us through the maze of life. He will help us know what to do when we face problems and tough decisions; but only when we take time to ask Him in prayer.

He has promised to instruct us, establish our thoughts, and guide our steps. *"In all your ways acknowledge Him, and He shall direct your paths."* *(Proverbs 3:6)*

"Your ears shall hear a word behind you, saying, 'This is the way, walk in it,' whenever you turn to the right hand or whenever you turn to the left." Isaiah 30:21

If you are prayerful, God will inspire you with good ideas. Jesus will prevent some problems from happening by warning you in advance and give you solutions to others.

"Whoever listens to Me will dwell safely, and will be secure, without fear of evil." (Proverbs 1:33)

Prayer certainly is vital in determining the perfect will of God for us, but not because it sorely gives us peace, but because it aligns us to the will and plan of God for our lives.

"Our Father who is in the heavens, your name be sanctified; Your kingdom come; Your will be done, as in heaven, so also on earth..." (Matthew 6:9)

The will of God is more important to us than any other. And we must constantly seek it through prayer. God created us, and He certainly knows us better.

He is willing to guide you in your everyday life, if you are willing, Pray!

❖ **Prayer ushers us into the heavenly secrets**

"CALL TO ME, and I will answer you, and show you great and mighty things, which you do not know." Jeremiah 33:3

The fact is, as per the above scripture, God has so many secrets and has hidden so much from us. And

He can only show these to us, only when we get to call upon Him.

Only when we call, that is when He will answer and show us great and mighty things we do not know. And this calling is only done through PRAYER!

This means if we do not pray, we will not be able to know the secrets of the Lord.

Another benefit of prayer is to touch the "throne of grace" to find grace for your timely help.

Hebrews 4:16 says, "Let us therefore come forward with boldness to the throne of grace that we may receive mercy and find grace for timely help."

What is grace? It is more than God's unmerited favor.

Grace is *"God in Christ as our supply and enjoyment, conveyed to us and realized through the bountiful supply of the Spirit of Jesus Christ (Philippians 1:19)"*

When we pray, we enter into the Holy of Holies and touch the throne of grace to enjoy the hidden secrets of God. We can also attain mercy through prayer.

When we pray we have access to a lot of information which we wouldn't have access to if we were not prayerful.

Some people have even gone to heaven and come back, because of their steadfast prayers.

Enjoying the flowing of God's grace in our prayer is more important than having our prayers answered.

❖ Prayer charges our spiritual lives

THE CHRISTIAN LIFE is like a tool or toy with a battery. Without being regularly charged, our "spiritual battery" will lack the power needed to carry out its intended functions.

Our prayer is our connection to the "charging station."

When we pray, our "spiritual battery" is charged with the heavenly current.

Revelations 22:1 "And He showed me a river of water of life, bright as crystal, proceeding out of the throne of God and of the Lamb..."

This divine, flowing river proceeding from God's throne supplies the power to charge us whenever we pray. There is power and authority that comes with prayer.

Because of prayer, demons confess and are cast out of people though deliverance.

A prayer less person can never command a demon to confess and leave unless if they use magic.

A prayer less Christian is certainly a powerless Christian, or rather, a prayer less Christian' is not a Christian, how can one call themselves a follower of Christ if they do not imitate Him?'

Jesus prayed!

❖ **Prayer is fellowship with the Lord**

PRAYER IS the contact of our spirit with God's spirit. *John 4:24 "God is Spirit and those who worship Him must worship in truth and in spirit..."*

It's by prayer that we enter into fellowship with the Lord and become conscious of the fact that we are really one spirit with Him and that He is actually one spirit with us *(1 Corinthians 6:17).*

Through prayer, we learn the heart of our Heavenly Father.

King David, known as a man after God's own heart recorded many of his prayers to God in the *Book of Psalms.*

Prayerfulness is a reflection of one's relationship with God. If one is after His heart, they will definitely pray to Him.

❖ **Prayer renews us**

EPHESIANS 4:23 says, "And that you be renewed in the spirit of your mind and put on the new man..."

This means that whenever we contact the Lord as the Spirit with our spirit through prayer, this spirit spreads into our mind for our renewing.

In such a way we are being renewed for the new man.

This new man is Christ's Body today and will become the New Jerusalem for eternity *(Revelations 21:2).* How wonderful that we can be renewed for the new man by our prayer. What a benefit!

❖ **Prayer helps us understand the word of God better**

COLOSSIANS 3:16 *"Let the word of Christ dwell in you richly in all wisdom..."*

There are times that we try to read the word of God, and it doesn't make sense. The harder we try, the more we get confused and the more we feel it is far from us.

The bible says, *'in the beginning was the word, and the word was with God and the word was God'. (John 1:1)*

There is no how one can understand the word deeply without having regular communion with God. And this starts with prayer.

By being prayerful and reading the word of God, you not only gain some mental understanding from the Bible, but you're nourished with life element in God's Word. God's words become "spirit and life" to you *(John 6:63)*.

❖ Prayer makes us sensitive spiritually

PRAYER IS the necessary prerequisite for spiritual awakening. If you want to be more sensitive in the spirit, to have spiritual gifts manifest in your life, like carrying out deliverances, healings, miracles, prophecies, you have to pray!

❖ Prayer sharpens discernment

If you want to be able to discern between good and wrong, prayer is the tool.

The bible says we should test the spirits, because not all of the men and women of God are of Him, and to be able to test, one has to be prayerful.

(2 Peter 2) "But there were also false prophets among the people, even as there will be false teachers among you, who will secretly bring in destructive

heresies, even denying the Lord who bought them, and bring on themselves swift destruction.

And many will follow their destructive ways, because of whom the way of truth will be blasphemed. By covetousness they will exploit you with deceptive words; for a long time their judgment has not been idle, and their destruction does not slumber"

When one does not pray, they fall prey to these false prophets whom we have been warned about. And when we pray, we are able to discern between the true ones and the false ones.

The dangerous part about following false prophets is that they affect even our destiny of going to heaven. If God disowns them and we follow them, how can we be of God?

If one is of God, they will hear His voice, the fact that one has fallen prey to them means he is not of God and cannot hear His voice.

❖ Prayer connects us with other believers

(Luke 22:31-32); And the Lord said, "Simon, Simon! Indeed, Satan has asked for you, that he may sift you as wheat. But I have prayed for you, that your faith should not fail; and when you have returned to Me, strengthen your brethren."

(Ephesians 3:14-21) "For this reason I bow my knees to the Father of our Lord Jesus Christ, from whom the whole family in heaven and earth is named, that He would grant you, according to the riches of His glory, to be strengthened with might through His Spirit in the inner man, that Christ may

dwell in your hearts through faith; that you, being rooted and grounded in love, may be able to comprehend with all the saints what is the width and length and depth and height to know the love of Christ which passes knowledge; that you may be filled with all the fullness of God.

The above scriptures encourage us to pray with others and for others.

When the early Church gathered together in fervent prayer for Peter after he was imprisoned, an angel rescued him from his chains. *Acts 12*.

Stories continue to be told today of how God miraculously answers the faithful prayers of his people.

We must never cease praying with and for our brothers and sisters in the faith; for it is through prayer that God continues to transform the world.

❖ Prayer helps glorify God

WHEN WE PRAY, asking God to do something for us and He does it, it brings Him glory, we testify, and others can also join in praising Him.

John 18: 13 "Whatever you ask in my name, this I will do, that the Father may be glorified in the Son"

When we pray and God answers us, we become grateful and appreciate Him more. We recognize Him for who He is and what He has done for us. In doing so, we bring honor to the Lord. We also learn to adopt a positive mindset.

When we recognize through prayer how God has worked in our lives, we begin to become more grateful in other areas of our lives as well.

❖ **Prayer keeps us humble**

IT'S IMPOSSIBLE to meet a prayerful Christian who has pride.

"If my people, who are called by my name, will humble themselves and pray and seek my face and turn from their wicked ways, then I will hear from heaven, and I will forgive their sin and will heal their land."

(2 Chronicles 7:14)

When we regularly go to God in prayer, our attitude changes. We become more and more humble, not only before Him, but also before man.

The story of the prayers of the tax collector and the Pharisee in *Luke 18* shows how God honors humility. While it is tempting to place ourselves first, an active prayer life can help us have a proper perspective.

Prayer demonstrates our willingness to be humbled daily and depend on God to meet our needs. We admit our weakness and our neediness by turning to God in prayer.

As we pray in faith, we find God changing our attitudes about ourselves, about our situations and about others.

❖ **Prayer instills a positive outlook on life**

WHEN YOU ARE in constant prayer, you will have a more positive outlook on life because you will be able to see things through the eyes of faith. For *we do not walk by sight but by faith. 2 Corinthians 5:7*

Once you have committed a matter to God in prayer, you can then have the assurance that He will take care of it in accordance with His will and this is faith.

That helps you fight against worry and view things more optimistically. *"We know that all things work together for good to those who love God." Romans 8:28*

Daily issues affect our stress levels and mood.

Daily prayer helps us look forward to a better tomorrow.

By being thankful for every day and every day to come praying changes one's outlook on life as a whole.

It also eliminates worry and anxiety.

By being prayerful we become hopeful, even in seemingly hopeless situations. Through prayer we do not give up easily.

We also become more confident in God.

There is what we call self-confidence and what is called Christ-Centered Confidence.

Self-confidence is trusting and believing in ourselves, but Christ Centered confidence is believing in the power and the ability of God in and through us. We therefore as children of God, should seek Christ centered confidence - it is much higher than self-confidence..

❖ Prayer triggers the release of the Holy Spirit

I HAVE NEVER heard of anyone who received the Holy Spirit without prayer.

Usually it is either one receives Him while praying themselves or while someone is praying for them.

Acts 1:14 "They all joined together constantly in prayer, along with the women and Mary the mother of Jesus, and with his brothers.

The Holy Spirit was poured down at Pentecost and many were baptized with the Holy Spirit. Everyone wants baptism of the Holy Spirit, unfortunately most fail to realize that it has to be preceded with a lot of prayer."

All revivals take place as a result of prayer.

Even in the above-mentioned scripture, the Holy Spirit was poured down as a result of prayer.

(Acts 8:15-17)' When they arrived, they prayed for them that they might receive the Holy Spirit, because the Holy Spirit had not yet come upon any of them;

they had simply been baptized into the name of the Lord Jesus.

Then Peter and John placed their hands on them, and they received the Holy Spirit.'

Even to this day, there is no different way to receive the Holy Spirit other than through prayer.

❖ Prayer helps overcome temptation

WE CAN USE prayer as an instrument to overcome sin and temptation.

(Matthew 26:41) "Watch and pray so that you will not fall into temptation. The spirit is willing, but the flesh is weak."

Many times, as people we find ourselves being tempted to go against the will and Word of God.

Sometimes we yield to temptations but yielding to temptations always results in sin.

Yet the wages of sin are undesirable.

Prayer is one of the tools available for use when faced with temptations.

When the world, the flesh, and the devil all press in on us in the same situation, we are in serious trouble but when we pray, we will stand.

The hour that Jesus and the disciples faced especially was as such in *Luke 22:53*. The eleven disciples were troubled and confused about all they had seen and heard regarding Jesus.

Jesus knew the temptations before His disciples, their reaction to His capture, His trials, His mockery, the denial, His Crucifixion, His death.

Also, satan wanted to destroy God's plan of salvation by tempting Jesus to avoid the cross.

Herod's kingdom, representing the world, wanted to get rid of Jesus so that they could continue in their place of power and prestige.

There were internal temptations and conflict that Jesus faced that made the cross reprehensible to Him. The disciples wrestled with fear and confusion.

This was an extremely intense trial. But Jesus prayed, to the point that His sweat became like blood.

Intense temptations - intense prayers!

If we want to overcome the trials and temptations that hit us, we must learn from our Lord Jesus Christ, He prayed in the midst of temptations.

When you face temptation, prayer is what will see you through.

We should always see prayer as a first option when facing temptation, not the last option after yielding to temptation.

If we would pray more, we would yield less to temptations, sin less and avoid the pain that comes with sin..

❖ **Prayer is a weapon of spiritual warfare**

MANY TIMES, when there is an incoming spiritual war in my life or the lives of my loves ones, the Holy Spirit instructs me to get into prayers.

I have found myself engaged in intense, rough spiritual warfare, and it is only through prayer, that I knew I would win.

And it is through praying, that I am continuously victorious even to this day.

To me, prayer is a major weapon in fighting my spiritual battles.

(Ephesians 6 11-18) "Put on the full armor of God, so that you can take your stand against the devil's schemes. For our struggle is not against flesh and blood, but against the rulers, against the authorities, against the powers of this dark world and against the spiritual forces of evil in the heavenly realms.

Therefore, put on the full armor of God, so that when the day of evil comes, you may be able to stand your ground, and after you have done everything, to stand.

Stand firm then, with the belt of truth buckled around your waist, with the breastplate of righteousness in place, and with your feet fitted with the readiness that comes from the gospel of peace.

In addition to all this, take up the shield of faith, with which you can extinguish all the flaming arrows of the evil one. Take the helmet of salvation and the sword of the Spirit, which is the word of God.

*And **pray** in the Spirit on all occasions with all kinds of prayers and requests. With this in mind, be alert and always keep on praying for all the Lord's people."*

The life of a Christian is not a walk in the park; it is a battlefield.

Do not be deceived to believe that for you to be qualified as a true Christian you must not have challenges or attacks, if our master Jesus Christ had them, and yet we are His servants, we certainly should face them too..

But in all these, the weapon of prayer diffuses Satan's fortress. Hell's gates cannot prevail where there is prayer. It is the cannon, reducing the wall to rubble so that the troops can go through.

Many times, the devil may win ONLY because of neglecting of prayer on our side.

Prayer is key to fighting spiritual battles. Take advantage of it, use it, and be VICTORIOUS!!

❖ Prayer results in breakthrough

HANNAH PRAYED for a child and God granted her wish in *1 Samuel 1:9-20*.

Abraham's servant prayed to God, and God directed him to person who should be wife to his master's son and heir *(Gen. 24:10-20)*.

Jacob prayed to God, and God inclined the heart of his irritated brother, so that they met in peace and friendship *(Gen. 32:24-30; 33:1-4)*.

Samson prayed to God, and God showed him a well where he quenched his burning thirst, and so lived to judge Israel *(Judges 15:18-20).*

David prayed, and God defeated the counsel of Ahithophel *(2 Samuel 15:31; 16:20-23; 17:14-23).*

Daniel prayed, and God enabled him both to tell Nebuchadnezzar his dream and to give the interpretation of it *(Daniel 2: 16-23).*

Esther and Mordecai prayed, and God defeated the purpose of Haman, and saved the Jews from destruction *(Esther 4:15-17; 6:7, 8).*

The believers in Jerusalem prayed, and God opened the prison doors and set Peter at liberty when Herod had resolved upon his death *(Acts 12:1-12).*

Elijah prayed and the fire of the LORD fell, and consumed the burnt sacrifice, and the wood, and the stones, and the dust, and licked up the water that was in the trench- *1 King 18:36-38.*

Elisha prayed and God raised the Shunammite son that was dead- *2 King 4:32-35*

They are many examples in the bible where the people of God prayed, and God answered their prayers and these should be motivation enough to build our faith in God to start praying earnestly unto Him.

The evidence is there, taking a stand in prayer is your choice!

❖ Prayer results in spiritual maturity

"Brothers, I could not address you as spiritual, but as worldly as infants in Christ. I gave you milk, not solid food, for you were not yet ready for solid food.

In fact, you are still not ready, for you are still worldly. For since there is jealousy and dissension among you, are you not worldly? Are you not walking in the way of man?" (1 Corinthians 3:1-3)

The above scripture acknowledges that when one is worldly, they are still infants in Christ, this is regardless of how many years one has been going to church, or how active one is in church, this does not exclude church leaders who are carnal - as much as they are carnal, they are spiritual babies despite their positions.

Where there is jealousy, competitions, comparisons, emotions, divisions and gossip in church; there, the world is, and where worldly traits are, there is infancy.

When a person gets born again, they still have a mentality and a way of doing things, including speaking, in a worldly or carnal manner.

But for them to change, it takes time; for them to learn to speak in a Godly way, or behave in a different way, it will not happen over night, not even a year is enough.

Hence, when one is born again, even though they may go to church and be committed, certain worldly traits may be found in them, and as much as they have such, they are considered to be babies in the things of the Kingdom of God.

Now, to grow from that level to another level until one reaches a higher level, to a point of maturity where worldly traits will no longer be found in such, prayer should be made the central and most important part of such a person's lifestyle.

It is impossible for one to grow spiritually without a regular, consistent prayer life.

At the end, it is impossible for a prayerful person to walk in the ways of man!!

If you are carnal, worldly, emotional, and judgmental; check your prayer life....

If you want to mature spiritually, pray without ceasing....

CHAPTER 4

WHERE TO START

1.   Time and place

YOU CAN PRAY anytime and anywhere.

Jesus met a woman beside a well who thought we all had to go to a particular place to pray and worship, as God's people had prayed in the Old Testament *(John 4:20)*.

But Jesus says to her, *"Woman, believe me, the hour is coming when neither on this mountain nor in Jerusalem will you worship the Father.*

The hour is coming, and is now here, when the true worshipers will worship the Father in spirit and truth" *(John 4:21)*.

117

Prayer is no longer focused in a place, but in the Spirit *(Ephesians 6:18).*

We should absolutely pray spontaneously whenever and wherever the Holy Spirit prompts us.

As Christians, we are free to pray anywhere, unfortunately, this freedom to pray anywhere, often leads us to praying nowhere. And this is an error!

Therefore, pick a consistent time and place when you can be alone. It might be in the morning at home, or during a long commute, or over your lunch break, or at a convenient time in the evening.

The times and places can be different for different people - one of the stunning blessings Jesus brought, but it should still be consistent for you regardless of the differences.

When it comes to prayer, what will eventually bring breakthrough is your heart, persistency and consistency.

2. Listen before you speak

ONE IMPORTANT THING to learn about prayer is that it is a conversation. Just as God speaks to us in His Word, He is also listening when we pray, on the other side of prayer.

On any given day, God may choose to move or "speak" in some unexpected way through his Spirit, bringing something to our mind, altering some circumstance, saying something through a friend. Listen and be attentive always.

Most importantly, God speaks to us through His Word.

"All Scripture is breathed out by God" 2 Timothy *3:16.*

Before praying, read a verse from the Bible. Those words from God are *"living and active, sharper than any two-edged sword, piercing to the division of soul and of spirit, of joints and of marrow, and discerning the thoughts and intentions of the heart"* Hebrews *4:12.*

Therefore, let God speak first before you speak. Let Him have the first word.

Put His living and active words into your ears, mind or heart and let them shape and inspire what you say back to Him.

When you do this, you will be shocked as to what you have been missing by not giving God an ear.

The fact is, God speaks all the time, as some people say, the way God speaks, is comparable to a radio station.

Not switching to its signal does not mean it is not there nor does it mean no one is speaking at the studio.

To be able to hear what the presenter says, or which music is playing, one has to switch to the station.

Even God speaks to us all the time, it is written, *"For God speaks in one way and in another, yet no one notices. " (Job 33:14)*

Unfortunately, this is what most Christians are doing even today.

May God give us a listening ear in the Mighty name of Jesus Christ!

3. **Prioritize the spiritual**

MANY TIMES, we focus on praying for our physical life, for those going through challenges, and we end up giving less attention to the spiritual life.

This can be our spiritual lives or the spiritual lives of those we feel a need to pray for.

It is not wrong by any means to focus on physical life only but if we take that mentality into prayer, we may only ever pray for physical or circumstantial needs.

Of course, physical needs are important, but they are less important in comparison to our spiritual needs.

Have you ever wondered about a person who is being prayed for every other day or Sunday at church, but their circumstance does not change?

Sometimes it is because we focus on the result of our lack of prayer, than on our actual lack of prayer and a genuine relationship with God.

*In Matthew 6:33, we are to seek **first** the Kingdom of God and His righteousness, and everything would then be added unto us.*

This means we should prioritize God first and His righteousness.

These as a result, will then influence what happens to us in the natural world or physically. Life is mainly about unseen realities.

The spiritual life dictates what happens in the physical.

If at all we desire a change in our physical lives, we need to work on our spiritual lives first.

4. **Don't be afraid to stop and pray**

ONE DAY I was driving to work, I was with some other people in the car, as we were deep in conversations.

I then felt a strong urge to pray, immediately I started praying, I did not understand why I had to pray, it did not make sense to me, but I prayed nonetheless.

After about 5 minutes, there was this big truck driving really slowly on the road which we were approaching, and many cars were overtaking it, it was in the morning and everyone was in a hurry to get to work on time.

Now it was my turn to overtake it, the moment I got into the other lane, the truck lost control and swayed between both lanes, in shock I drove back to my lane and applied brakes, the truck had two tyre bursts!!

And through prayer, God saved us from a possible terrible accident.

Another time we were driving with my husband, on the way I felt a prompt to pray, of which I did, it was dawn, and we were driving on the country side.

As I was in prayer, I looked ahead and there was an animal right in the middle of the road, I warned my husband, and he managed to control the car not to hit the animal. He then confessed that, though he was driving, he did not see the animal, until I warned him...!

When you feel the impulse to pray, seize it and pray. You may not be praying for yourself at that moment, but for your loved one who is about to be in trouble, or accident and your prayer may avert that.

Take the urge to pray as a prompting of the Holy Spirit; *Romans 8:26 "Likewise the Spirit helps us in our weakness. For we do not know what to pray for as we ought, but the Spirit himself intercedes for us with groanings too deep for words."*

Satan certainly will not encourage you to pray, do not give in to him, imagine what would have happened in the above circumstances if I had ignored those promptings to pray?

These are spirit-led prayers, and their results are always amazing. Indeed, God looks out for us; He never sleeps nor slumbers.

Any discouragement to pray is not of God. Even if you can see someone saying they are pastors or prophets but discouraging you to pray, know then that they are the tool of the enemy! This is, because when the devil wants to attack anyone, he starts with affecting their prayer life negatively.

Also, when someone asks you to pray for them, do it right there and then, at that very moment; do not say you will do it later. Even over a telephone conversation, do it!

We live busy lives, most of the times we promise to pray with people going through hardships but end up forgetting, because the moment we finish conversing with them, there are a million things in mind to do.

It usually does not take long to pray for such but does surely makes a difference; not only in their circumstance, but also in you.

Do not let them go until you pray for them!!!

5. **Identify your prayer pattern**

WHEN IT COMES to praying for the lives of your loved ones or people around you, you will have to prioritize some people over others, otherwise, you will do nothing but pray.

For me daily I pray for my loved ones, my marriage, children, husband, small group, nation, etc.

This however should not keep us from praying for the random people, friends we meet daily.

The most important thing to do for anyone is to pray for them. Even our children, the best gifts we can give to them, is to impart a prayer life upon them, and to pray for their future, **now**.

It is vital to maintain a particular prayer pattern and circle but we should be flexible enough to accommodate more prayers for people outside it.

6. **Ask whatever you wish; literally anything!**

IF WE ARE HONEST, many of us lack courage and imagination in our prayer lives.

We have a tiny little box of routine things we are willing to ask God for, and we take on everything else, our questions, our frustrations, our dreams, on our own.

We assume God is interested in some things in our lives and is not interested in some.

To the point that we wait to pray about something until it becomes serious enough or unbearable for us to handle.

By doing this, we deprive ourselves of His massive, never-ending mercy and power in different areas of our lives and world.

"Is anything too hard for the LORD?" (Genesis 18:14)

We pray to a God *"who is able to do far more abundantly than all that we ask or think" (Ephesians 3:20)*

Jesus says, "If you have faith like a grain of mustard seed, you will say to this mountain move from here to there,' and it will move, and nothing will be impossible for you" (Matthew 17:20)

To prove that the word of God is real, I have at some point asked God to make my husband a very patient person, and God being faithful to His word, has granted me exactly that.

One would have thought; how can I pray for this? Is it even possible?

Can God really make a person patient? To me, yes, I believed it, I prayed for it, and God granted it.

I would not have prayed for it, if I did not believe it, and God would not have granted me this, if I had not prayed for it; it all starts with **faith**!

If I had not taken a step of asking for it from God, my husband would not be this patient.

As human beings we have a tendency of limiting God to our human limitations, forgetting that He is way above us.

Pray for anything!

I have seen one man of God praying for women who were overweight to lose weight and they lost the weight right there, standing on top of a bathroom scale and the readings were going down, and the skirts becoming loose that they had to hold the skirts with their hands least they fall down and leave them naked!!

I have seen people who were suffering from hypertension being instantly healed, the machine readings going down to normal right at that moment, right in the eyes of man, through prayer!

Do we have enough faith to think God can do anything for us? Even the things we have never imagined?

Someone once said, can God make a house for a person, my answer was, and still is, YES He can!

God cares about everything in our lives, Paul says, *"Do not be anxious about anything" this includes your health, your finances, your children - "but in everything by prayer and supplication, with thanks*

*giving let your requests be made known to God"
(Philippians 4:6)*

The above scripture says, Anything and everything! Every day!

Do not be afraid to pray big, bold, daring prayers, God can do it.

Also never ever think there is a small prayer, before God, all prayer is important.

One day I bought an iron, with an expectation that it will last many years, to my surprise, after two months, the iron went dead.

I was disappointed and hurt, especially looking at the amount of money I have spent on it. With hope, every time I am supposed to iron my clothes, I would plug it first and switch it on to see if it won't work, but still nothing.

This happened for about three months. Until one day I plugged it, it did not switch on, and I said to myself that instead of using a different iron, I am going to pray for it.

The moment I said this in my heart, before I could even lay my hands on it, the iron switched on!

Do not limit God to think there are things He can do or things He cannot do.

Nothing in this earth is hard for Him. No situation is impossible for Him to change! Pray for anything and everything.

If it steals your peace, pray about it; if it hurts pray about it...

If you do not pray for anything, how will you have and receive?

7. **Be persistent**

JESUS KNEW THAT somehow we would lose heart in prayer, specifically that we would pray for things for long enough that we would start to question if God was listening or might ever answer.

However, He did not want us to lose heart or give up. He wanted us to keep asking, keep pleading, keep praying.

He went on and told His disciples a story about a widow seeking justice from a judge, "who neither feared God nor respected man." She pled and pled with him in *Luke 18:1-8.*

For a while the judge refused, but afterward he said to himself, *'Though I neither fear God nor respect man, yet because this widow keeps bothering me, I will*

135

give her justice, so that she will not beat me down by her continual coming.'

And the Lord said, *"Hear what the unrighteous judge says. And will not God give justice to his elect, who cry to him day and night? Will he delay long over them?" Luke 18:4–8*

God knows what is best for you, and He is listening. Don't be afraid to pray and ask Him, again and again and again until He grants you what you desire!!

The widow got rewarded for her persistence by an unrighteous judge. How much more will God listen to you when you ask and ask and ask? If the unrighteous judge could not ignore her, how much more will our heavenly Father hear us who is righteous?

Another illustration of persistence is in *Matthew 15:22* where a woman of Canaan came to Christ stating: "... Have mercy on me ... my daughter is grievously vexed with a devil..."

Interestingly, Jesus did not respond to her request immediately, but she did not give up, she kept on asking; only after her persistence then her request was granted.

Our Lord's attitude was intended to test the woman's faith, which was rewarded by the miraculous healing of the woman's daughter.

Thus, we may conclude that often our prayers are not answered immediately, simply because God may be testing our faith.

God may desire that we repeat with persistence our request for a specific need before He answers that need.

Therefore, be persistent, Keep praying!!

Jesus asked *"Which one of you, if his son asks him for bread, will give him a stone? Or if he asks for a fish, will give him a serpent? If you then, who are evil, know how to give good gifts to your children, how much more will your Father who is in heaven give good things to those who ask him!" (Matthew 7:9–11)*

From the above, God wants assures us that we can trust Him with anything.

He assures us that what we ask of Him, He will do it, just like our earthly fathers do.

Therefore, God is waiting for you to ask from Him, do not give up!

Do not be afraid to ask, again and again and again.

It is important to note that even though God assures to answer us, sometimes God forces us to wait for an answer to our prayers in order to teach us patience and perseverance.

Sometimes we ask for something that is not yet in God's timing for our lives.

Sometimes we ask for something that is not God's will for us, and He says "no."

Prayer is not only about us presenting our requests to God; it is also about giving God a chance to present His will to our hearts and lives.

Keep on asking, keep on knocking, and keep on seeking until God grants your request or convinces you that your request is not His will for you.

8. **Pray simply**

WE MIGHT THINK that we have to pray passionate, persuasive words for God to hear us, but in reality He listens to each and every one of our prayers, even the ones we do in heart.

Most importantly, allow the Holy Spirit to lead you, He can give you the words, the issues to pray for, and even the language to use in prayer, let loose and allow Him to take over and guide you.

"In the same way the Spirit also helps our weakness; for we do not know how to pray as we should, but the Spirit Himself intercedes for us with groanings too deep for words; and He who searches the hearts knows what the mind of the Spirit is, because He intercedes for the saints according to the will of God."
(Romans 8:26-27)

9. **Read the Word**

HAVE YOU EVER had a one-sided conversation with someone who talked continually without listening to you? The conversation did not go very well or far, did it?

We do the same thing to God when we pray without reading the Bible, His eternal letter of love and wisdom to each one of us on earth.

Reading Scripture helps us get to know God.

It brings life to our prayers and to us.

If you want to have a more effective conversation with God, read the Scripture and use the scripture in your prayers.

The results of such prayers will shock you. Such prayers are effective always.

10. **Keep a prayer book**

I KEEP A prayer book with me, and this has been the case for so many years since I was at varsity.

I make a list of my prayer requests, their dates, and the prayers corresponding to the requests.

I even write down if the request is accompanied with fasting or not.

What I have learnt from this is that God is faithful, and keeps His promises, there are times I revisit my old prayer books and I get shocked when I realize that most, if not all of the things I have now, I once took time to pray for them..!

A prayer book builds faith when you look back over your petitions and recall God's answers.

It also helps us count our blessings, and when we realize how faithful God has been through years, we appreciate, love and trust Him more..

When I was at varsity, I prayed for a man who shall be my husband, I told God everything I wanted in that man; now looking back at my prayers, which I had written down in my prayer book and looking at my husband, I get excited at how faithful God has been to me. He gave me exactly what I asked for!

Had I not written these down, I would have forgotten about this request that I had made to God.

However, I only remembered this request, after years into my marriage, when I was going through my old stuff and found that old prayer book.

11. **Make Prayer an integral part of your day**

"REJOICE ALWAYS, pray without ceasing, give thanks in all circumstances;" (1 Thessalonians 5:16-17)

One can ask, but is it really possible to pray without ceasing?

Try starting and end your day with prayer. Lift up short prayers to God as often as you can throughout your day.

Pray over your schedule, family, friends, food, bless God, worship Him, recite His word. Ask God to help you with your to-do list.

When you hear a troubling news report, lift the situation up to God.

Say a prayer for your spouse or child as you give him or her a hug.

Pray for the person you are talking to. These may look like a lot of work, but they keep one focused on God, make life easier, gives peace, changes circumstances, changes the future, even though you may not realize it.

I have once told a friend of mine that if God could open our spiritual eyes for just a minute so that we see the wars, the demons, evil beings fighting us, the traps set for us, we would request Jesus to come!

These little prayers are worth it.

Start today and see what happens in your life and in the lives of those around you.

12. **Pray expectantly**

PRAYER BECOMES A lifeless exercise when we're not expecting answers.

Jesus invites us to expect God to work.

"Ask, and it will be given to you; seek, and you will find; knock, and it will be opened to you."(Matthew 7:7)

How much more exciting can prayer become when we keep our eyes open to watch for God's answers? Sometimes I wonder how many answers we miss because we do not really expect God to respond.

Remember *"Devote Yourselves to Prayer, being watchful and thankful." (Colossians 4:2)*

Do not get discouraged, pray and watch for God's answers, so you can thank Him.

He might answer differently than you expect, but His answer will always be better than what you had in mind.

Sometimes when I pray to God to do something for me in the future, I thank God for it now...

It might not make sense, but the things of the spirit are foolishness to those of this world.

I went to Japan to do my Master's Degree in Public Finance in 2017. Before I left for school, I started thanking God for my academic excellence, for my perfect stay there, I even thanked God, for my successful completion of my studies and my graduation. I also thanked God for my safe return back to my home country.

All these, I did them before I set foot in Japan! Before I started going to class...!

Without faith, we cannot please God, we should not walk by sight but by faith, we should live our lives in a way that we do not wait for things to happen first and then we say thank you Lord.

We can start thanking God for what we have asked of Him.

I know of a couple who could not conceive a child. They had tried for so many years to conceive but failed dismally.

They have done everything medically possible but the treatments did not work.

Until one day, they decided to do everything by faith. They prayed, then went to the shops to buy clothes for their first born, they did not care what people thought, they knew that it may seem like foolishness, but that is the only way they can access God's grace and mercy, FAITH!

After that, God did not only bless them with one child, but many!

CHAPTER 5

HOW SHOULD WE PRAY?

SOMEONE ONCE ASKED me, "how should we pray?"

Is it best to pray standing up, sitting down, kneeling, or bowing down?

Should our hands be open, closed, or lifted up to God? Do our eyes need to be closed when we pray?

Is it better to pray in a church building or out in nature?

Should we pray in the morning when we get up or at night before we go to bed?

Are there certain words we need to say in our prayers?

How do we begin our prayers?

What is the proper way to close a prayer?

These questions, and others, are common questions asked about prayer. What is the proper way to pray?

My question then became, **does any of the above things even matter?**

Some Christians believe that if we do not say exactly the right things, or pray in the right position, God will not hear and answer our prayers.

This is completely unbiblical: the bible is our standard of life and in everything we do, we should make reference to it, and as far as I know, none of these is there in the bible.

Why do Christians like limiting themselves? Or rather, limiting God?

God does not answer our prayers based on when we pray, where we are, what position our body is in, or in what order we word our prayers.

We are told in *1 John 5:14-15* to have confidence when we come to God in prayer, knowing He hears us and will grant whatever we ask as long as it is in His will.

Similarly, *John 14:13-14* declares, *"And I will do whatever you ask in my name, so that the Son may bring glory to the Father. You may ask me for anything in my name, and I will do it."*

According to these and many other Scriptures, God answers prayer requests based on whether they are asked according to His will and in the name of Jesus to bring glory to the Father.

God will answer all prayers with the gift of His peace in our hearts.

The proper way to pray is to pour out our hearts to God, being honest, sincere and open with God, as He already knows us better than we know ourselves.

We are to present our requests to God, keeping in mind that God knows what is best and will not grant a request that is not His will for us.

We are to express our love, gratitude, and worship to God in prayer without worrying about having just the right words to say.

God is not interested in the eloquence of our words.

The proper way to pray is to express our hearts to God.

Sitting, standing, or kneeling; hands open or closed; eyes opened or closed; in a church, at home, or outside; in the morning or at night—these are all side issues, subject to personal preference, conviction, and appropriateness.

God's desire is for prayer to be a real and personal connection between Himself and us.

Prayer is most effective when we strive to be clean and obedient, with worthy motives, and are willing to do what He asks.

Humble, genuine, trusting prayer changes things.

When you pray, do not worry about posture, words, place, etc., just talk to your loving, caring, compassionate and understanding Father.

You are His precious child whom He loves perfectly and wants to help.

As you pray, remember, He is listening.

A key to improved prayer is to learn to ask the right questions.

Consider changing from asking for the things you want; to honestly seek what He wants for you. Then as you learn His will, pray that you will be led to have the strength to accept and fulfill it.

Pray even when you have no desire to pray.

The moment you feel like not praying, keep this in mind; that is when you mostly need and have to pray. When it comes to prayer, do not entertain laziness. The first thing that the devil does to attack a prayerful Christian is to make then lazy to pray, when you feel like that, you are definitely under spiritual attack and need to up your game, least you fall for the tricks of the enemy by prayerlessness.

Again, never feel you are too unworthy to pray.

No matter what you have done, do not let guilt, or other people doubt your prayers, because God never does that.

Should you ever feel disconnected from our Heavenly Father, for any reason, take it as a reason to pray more and reconcile with Him. Plead for reconciliation, forgiveness, He is waiting.

Often when we pray for help with a significant matter, our Heavenly Father will give us gentle promptings that require us to think, exercise faith, work, at times struggle, then receive.

This is a step-by-step learning process that enables us to discern spirit inspired answers.

Again, as you begin to pray, whether it is just walking somewhere during the day, in church or in your room, take a moment to acknowledge whose presence you are in.

"Be still and know that I am God" (Psalms 46:11)

"I am with you always." (Matthew 28:18)

"I will never leave you nor forsake you" (Deuteronomy 31:6)

Also, when praying, be yourself: Many people think holiness is unattainable, and that to pray we need to look in a certain way or be in a certain posture.

The reality is that we were created to be in communion with God, and He desires to be in a relationship with every one of us.

He doesn't want you to be a carbon copy of anyone. You are fearfully and wonderfully made, unique and different.

He created you with your own gifts and passions and wants to shine through you uniquely in them. Come to Him as you are and let Him transform you into what He wants you to be!

'Teach us to pray' (Luke 11:1)

Jesus' apostles asked Him these words, and that conversation resulted in what we call the 'The Lord's Prayer'.

If His own apostles asked Jesus to teach them how to pray, how much more should we ask Him to teach us to pray!

If you do not know how to pray, ask Him, the one who wants us to pray. Ask Him to help you and He will. The good thing about our Father is that you can come to Him with all your weakness and He will never look you down or let you down. Pray to the Heavenly Father: prayer should not be made to any man, angels, demons, idols or anything else other than the one true and living God.

Why should you put your trust and make many prayers to something that was created by God, man or to someone that is a mere man?

Anything you pray to, make sure it is good enough to be your God, make sure it can heal you when you're sick or raise you from the dead.

Make sure it is not created or equal to any man or machine upon the face of this world.

Make sure it, like angels and demons who were created, it was not created to serve mankind.

God is the only one who deserves the right to demand prayers and it is Him that will answer. The scripture below says it all.

Jeremiah 33:2-3 "This is what the Lord says, He who made the earth, the Lord who formed it and established it, the Lord is His name: Call to me and I will answer you and tell you great and unsearchable things you do not know.'

Prayers should also be made in the name of Jesus and no other name. The moment you use a different name; you disqualify your prayers from being answered by the Heavenly Father.

If God says, this is how you have to do it, then that is how you have to do it.

Doing the opposite will not get His attention.

John 15:16 'You did not choose me, but I chose you and appointed you so that you might go and bear fruit—fruit that will last—and so that whatever you ask in my name the Father will give you"

Additionally, never doubt God: *"if any of you lacks wisdom, you should ask God, who gives generously to all without finding fault, and it will be given to you. But when you ask, you must believe and not doubt, because the one who doubts is like a wave of the sea, blown and tossed by the wind. That person should not expect to receive anything from the Lord. Such a person is double-minded and unstable in all they do." (James 1:5-8)*

Our prayers are hindered when we doubt God. The Lord requires total belief and trust in His word. To question God's word, is to call Him a liar. Rather, believe in Him and His word.

Furthermore, prayer should be in line with the word of God because faith in His word is a guarantee for answer to prayer.

Sometimes we go to God and ask Him for something that is positively promised in His word, but we do not totally believe and expect it to happen.

Such an attitude would definitely hinder answers to our prayers.

God and His word can never fail, never change and never disappoint. He that doubt's God's word is unstable and can't obtain answers from the Lord.

In the end, prayers can be long or short, petitions or praises, questions or affirmations. Prayers can be for oneself or for another.

They can be from a joyous heart, a downcast heart, a repentant heart, or a broken heart, but all prayer should be in reverence of God and with a desire to submit to His will.

CHAPTER 6

HOW OFTEN SHOULD ONE PRAY?

PRAYING ALWAYS with all prayer and supplication in the Spirit and watching thereunto with all perseverance and supplication for all saints. — **Ephesians 6:18**

To pray regularly requires a certain level of discipline.

Unfortunately, most people are on-off when it comes to prayer.

They are faithful for a while, but then they fall out of prayer because they are too tired to get up early, or they become distracted by other things, or because they are not getting the answer soon enough.

But the above scripture clearly tells us that prayer is not optional for a Christian who is serious about his or her spiritual life.

According to this scripture, believers are to make prayer a top priority. Some people say they really want to pray, but they are very busy and hence lack time to pray, my believe is that if truly one desires in their heart to pray, they can and will find the time for it.

You can start by asking God to help you create time to pray.

Ask Him to help you manage your time wisely.

Remember you can ask Him for anything!

'And I say unto you, Ask, and it shall be given you; seek, and ye shall find; knock, and it shall be opened unto you. For everyone that asks receives; and he that seeks finds; and to him that knocks it shall be opened' (Luke 11:9,10).

He is our Father and desires to give us freely all things we ask for. He is waiting...

CHAPTER 7

DOES GOD ANSWER PRAYERS?

THE BIBLE ASSURES us that our Almighty God answers the prayers of His faithful servants, but it also gives reasons why He does not listen to some prayers.

The bible also tells us that wickedness will cause God to hide His face from us and do not answer our prayers.

For example, at a time when violence was rampant in ancient Israel, God directed His prophet Isaiah to tell the people: *"Although you offer many prayers, I am not listening; your hands are filled with blood." (Isaiah 1:15)*

Clearly, those who show contempt for God's laws or pray with improper motives cannot expect to be heard by God.

"When you do ask, you do not receive because you are asking for a wrong purpose, so that you may spend it on your fleshly desires" (James 4:3)

Some people come before God for prayer because they are in competition with another person, be rest assured, God will not give a 'yes' to that prayer.

On the other hand, the Bible states: *"No matter what we ask according to His will, He hears us." 1 John 5:14*

This does not mean that God will give us everything we ask for. The prerequisite is that it has to be according to His will. Also hearing does not imply answering.

Consider the case of the apostle Paul, who begged God **three times** to remove *"a thorn in the flesh."* *2 Corinthians 12:7, 8*

God clearly heard his cries, and I believe it was very frustrating for him!

Imagine that Paul had been given the gift of healing and had even performed a resurrection, yet he had to endure his own illness. *Acts 19 & 20*

At the end, what is comforting is that, even though the answer to his petitions did not take the form he wanted, Paul accepted God's response with gratitude. *2 Corinthians 12:9, 10*

King David asked: *"How long, O Jehovah, will you forget me? Forever?" (Psalm 13:1)*

But when that faithful man realized how often Jehovah had come to his rescue, David reaffirmed his trust in God. In the same prayer, David added: *"As for me, I trust in your loyal love." (Psalm 13:5)*

Just like David, God's worshippers today may have to persevere in prayer until they perceive God's response to their petitions.

There are many cases of the men and women who cried out to God in prayer and God did not answer. However, there are also many He answered positively, Hannah could not have any children as she was barren *(1 Samuel 1),* we are told that when she prayed to God He answered her prayers and she conceived and born a child by the name of Samuel who later became a Prophet and Judge of Israel, not only that, but she had more children after this.

Also, sometimes when you approach God with pride and do not humble yourself before the sovereign ruler He will not answer positively to your prayers *'Though the Lord is on high, Yet He regards the lowly; But the proud He knows from afar.' (Psalms 138:6)*

Do you know that hating someone is just like committing murder in the eyes of *God "Whoever hates his brother is a murderer, and you know that no murderer has eternal life abiding in him" 1 John 3:15.*

If you are a murder and come to God in prayer, how do you expect Him to answer?

Many of us have given up on praying because we believe that God did not answer our prayers. However, God always answers our prayer, it is either a yes, no, or not yet. God will **NOT** give you something that you are not ready for, or He is not ready to give you.

Just like a loving father will not always give his children everything they ask for because either they are not ready for it or it is not good for them; neither will God grant every request we make.

Of course our earthly father sometimes when they should have said yes, had said no, but God never makes that mistake. His yes is the right yes!

THINGS TO KEEP IN MIND WHEN PRAYING

❖

God will not always answer our way

MANY OF US have personally encountered a time or know of a time when we did not get what we desired even though we prayed.

But this does not mean prayer did not work. It is perhaps unfair to dismiss prayer because of those few stories when compared to the huge number of examples of when prayer certainly worked.

Prayer is a privilege, not an entitlement. God does not owe it to us to give us anything we pray for. We can fall into the mistake of thinking that if God does not answer our prayers, that God has somehow acted unfairly.

However, whenever God reaches into our world and transforms it on our behalf to answer our prayers God is being more than fair.

As I have already stated, and we already know, God does answer prayers and God answers prayers abundantly. Focus on what He has done, than on what He has not yet done..!

❖

Our prayers have to be aligned to His will

THROUGH PRAYER we should make sure that the requests we make of God are aligned with God's will, and not just our own. We also need to be very cautious about mixing the two.

Just because we really want something to be true does not mean it is God's will for our life.

Jesus gave us a model to pray and we should take that prayer to heart. When we pray, the heart of our prayers are meant to be "your will be done on earth as it is heaven", not "my will be done." If you feel that your prayer is in line with His will, then keep asking, do not give up.

The disciples were not praying according to God's will when they prayed with vindictiveness and revenge. They petitioned God thusly, *"Shall we command fire to come down from heaven and consume them?" Jesus answered, "You do not know what manner of spirit you are of" (Luke 9:54, 55).*

Job, in his sorrow, begged God to take his life away. What if God had answered such a prayer? Such praying was contrary to the will of God. The Word warns, *"Let not thy lip be hasty to utter a matter before the Lord." Ecclesiastes 5:2*

The unfortunate part is that we seem to know too much about what we want and too little about what God wants. Give Him a chance..

❖

God responds to our genuine needs

FOR GOOD REASONS, caring parents do not always give their children *what* they ask for *when* they ask for it. In a similar manner, God may not respond to our requests in the way we think He should or at the moment we expect.

But we can be confident that our Creator, as He did to the men and women in the bible and like a loving father, will respond to our genuine needs at the right time and in the right way.

❖

Some answers must be in God's timetable

THE BIBLE says that Almighty God shows favor to humble individuals *"in due time." 1 Peter 5:6*

So if there seems to be a delay in His answering our sincere requests, we need not see this as a lack of interest on Jehovah's part. Rather, with His vastly superior perspective, our caring Creator no doubt evaluates our petitions in the light of what He knows is best for us.

"Humble yourselves, therefore, under the mighty hand of God, so that He may exalt you in due time."
1 Peter 5:6

❖

His thoughts are not our thoughts

ISAIAH 55:8-9 "For My thoughts are not your thoughts, Nor are your ways My ways," says the Lord. "For as the heavens are higher than the earth, So are My ways higher than your ways, And My thoughts than your thoughts."

We sometimes do not fully understand the heart of God in this world, and as such, we will not always know why God always do what He does.

While we may not know, we can have resolute confidence in God. On a multitude of occasions God has graciously answered our prayers and we can have full faith that God is a God who listens to everything we pray, and God is a God who is actively at work in the world. That He has done it before, and will certainly do it again..

When we pray we ask the Lord of all to change things on our behalf. May we treat that task with the full gravity and seriousness that it deserves. May we learn to pray better, may what we pray be in God's will and may we pray boldly with confidence in Jesus Mighty name!

❖

God knows what is best for us

EVEN WHEN we feel that God is not answering our prayers, you can always know God is a God of love.

The Bible tells us He loves us: *John 3:16. '"For God so LOVED the world".......*

Jeremiah 31:3, "I have loved you with an everlasting love."

God created us and knows infinitely more than we know. He knows what is best for us, and what would not be good for us.

If you have children, when they were very small, sometimes they asked for things that would not be good for them or would harm them.

For good reasons sometimes, parents do not always give their children what they ask for, when they ask for it.

Parents give children what is best for them.

It is the same way in our prayers to God. God gives us what is best for us.

We are God's children and He gives us what is best for us, and at a time when it is best for us. Our lives must be right with God before He can answer our prayers.

His time, His will, God is a God of love, and He is interested in every detail of our lives. He hears our prayers and answers every sincere prayer if we meet His conditions. We must not expect that every answer will be "yes", since we are sinners and do not always ask what is best for us.

Sometimes His answer is "No' and sometimes it is "wait." *(Hebrew 10:36)*

We need to end each prayer with, "Not my will but Your will." Even if we are sincerely doing God's will, and to the best of our ability, following His will for us, He may see that it is best for us not for Him to say "yes" at this time.

We must continue trusting Him, regardless of His answer at the moment.

God's timetable is not the same as ours. He knows better than we do when is the best time for our prayers to be answered. *(Hebrews 6 :13-15).*

God is eternal and does not measure time as we do. Be patient.

2 Peter 3:8: "Beloved, do not forget this one thing, that with the Lord one day is as a thousand years, and a thousand years as one day."

In the story of Abraham, God promised a son to Abraham. But Abraham became impatient when Sarah did not bear him a son, so he took his wife's servant as his wife.

Abraham tried to solve the problem in his own way and the result was disastrous. We are still seeing the results of his mistake today.

God eventually answered his prayer at the time when He saw it was best for Abraham. For God to give us what we ask for, we must ask "according to His will."

Faith cannot take the place of "asking according to God's will." *1 John 5:14, "...if we ask anything according to His will, He hears us."*

If you do not ask according to God's will, it is not real faith in God.

If God's answer is "No" we still must be willing to wait patiently, and trust God to answer in his own way and in His timing.

Trust God, even though it may seem like prayer doesn't work. Even though it may seem like at the moment He is not near and has abandoned you. *Isaiah 41:9,10: "You whom I have taken from the ends of the earth, and called from its farthest regions, and said to you, you are my servant, I have chosen you, and have not cast you away.*

Fear not for I am with you; be not dismayed, for I am your God. I will strengthen you, Yes, I will help you, I will uphold you with My righteous right hand." If we have faith and sincerely trust God, we will not be concerned as to whether the answer is "wait" or the answer is "no" or "yes."

We must just trust and wait and see if God in His timing will see fit to answer as we have requested, or perhaps He has something better in mind for us.

Remember your prayer should end with *"Not my will, Lord, but Your will." (Luke 22:42).*

"Trust in the Lord with all thine heart; and lean not unto thine own understanding. In all thy ways acknowledge Him, and He shall direct thy paths." Proverbs 3:5,6.

Many doubts are seemingly caused when believers do not receive the answers to their prayers or other needs like they think they should.

In other words, uncertainty sometimes occurs when God does not act in the way that we think is required.

This is a tremendous principle for believers today to learn, too. When God's silence or the presence of pain and evil can be explained, so much the better.

But even when such cannot be figured out, we ought to trust God, for we have enough of a basis to do so.

After all, if man is finite, why do we frequently act as if we must be able to explain everything in the universe? At least this major principle should be garnered from the Book of Job.

After all, if even Jesus resigned Himself to the will of His Father, why shouldn't Christians learn to do the same? But, as we have seen, there are many other lessons that are also applicable to the issue of God's silence.

To this end we have endeavored to point out, initially, that it was common for believers in Scripture to both wonder why their prayers were not answered and to question God's silence, which sometimes lasted for long periods of time.

God answers many prayers according to the request, while believers have concluded that others have not been responded to according to their own judgements.

Using the experiences of Job and Abraham, we see that some believers have grown even during tough times. And like both of them, believers today can also resolve to trust the Lord even further, right during times of doubt and dismay.

One principle here is that, since we know enough about God in other crucial areas, we can trust Him even in those further instances where we cannot figure things out completely.

After all, I may not know why I am presently suffering, but this is still a world where God has raised Jesus from the dead. This is the world that He made, and He certainly has good plans for me.

Here we need to practice our faith during times of doubt, perhaps by directly affirming our belief to God during prayer or meditation.

Another helpful practice is to literally list our answers to prayer as they come about, thereby providing a ready list for times when we experience questions as to how much God answers our prayers.

Incidentally, such questions are more usually emotional in nature and so just such a list is helpful in confronting our own untruths which we tell ourselves.

And then, as Job and Abraham experienced, we can also witness the growth of our faith and the corresponding lessening of the grip of doubt.

The devil's final strategy in deceiving believers is to make them doubt the faithfulness of God in answering prayer, so that eventually, we stop praying altogether. Satan would have us believe God has shut His ears to our cry and left us to work things out for ourselves, but this is not true.

I believe the greatest tragedy in the church of Jesus Christ today is that, few people now believe in the power and effectiveness of prayer and yet they have tasted it.

Without meaning to blaspheme, multitudes of God's people can now be heard complaining, "I pray, but I get no answers. I have prayed so long, so hard, without any results. ''

All I want is to see a little evidence of God changing things. Things go on as usual - nothing happens. How long must I wait?"

They no longer visit the secret closet because they are convinced that their petitions, born in prayer, are somewhere miscarried at the throne.

Others are convinced that only Daniel, David, and Elijah types can get their prayers through to God.

In all honesty, many saints of God struggle with these thoughts - "If God's ear is open to my prayer, and I pray diligently, why is there such little evidence of His answering?"

Is there one certain prayer you have been praying for such a long time, and as yet it has not been answered?

Have even years gone by and still you wait, hoping, yet wondering?

Keep praying..

Do not charge God, as did Job, with being slothful; and unconcerned about our needs and petitions. Job complained, *"I cry unto thee and thou dost not hear me; I stand up, and though regards me not"* (Job 30:20).

His vision of God's faithfulness was clouded by his present difficulties, and he ended up accusing God of forgetting him and this is what we are doing even today as Christians. God rebuked him soundly for it.

It's time we Christians took an honest look at the reasons why our prayers are aborted. We can be guilty of charging God with neglect when all along our own behavior is responsible.

Our iniquities also separate us from God, the sin that we do when no one sees, lust in our hearts, hatred, forgiveness, etc., and they make Him not hear us when we call unto Him.

Isaiah 59:2 "But your iniquities have separated you from your God; your sins have hidden his face from you, so that he will not hear."

❖

It is possible to ask amiss

"YOU ASK AND receive not, because you ask amiss, that ye may consume it upon your lust" (James 4:3).

God will answer no prayer that would add to our honor or assist our temptations.

In the first place, God answers no prayer of a person who harbors lust in his or her heart. All answers are dependent on the plucking out of our hearts of the evil, the lust, and the besetting sins therein.

"If I regard iniquity in my heart, the Lord will not hear me" (Psalm 66:18).

The test of knowing whether or not our request is based on lust is very simple. **How we handle delays and denials is the clue.**

Prayers founded on lust demand hasty answers. If the lusting heart does not get the thing desired, quickly, it whimpers and cries, it swoons and faints - or it breaks out in a spell of murmuring and complaining, finally accusing God of deafness.

Wherefore have we fasted, say they, and thou seest not" (Isaiah 58:3).

The lustful heart cannot see God's glory in His denials and delays. Yet did God not get more glory by denying Christ's prayer to save His life, if possible, from death?

Shudder to think of where we would be today had God not denied that request.

God, in His justice, is obligated to delay or deny our prayers until they are purged of all selfishness and lust.

Could it be there is one simple reason why most of our prayers are hindered? Could it be a result of our ongoing flirtation with a lust or besetting sin?

Have we forgotten that only those with clean hands and pure hearts can set their feet on His holy hill?

Only a total forsaking of sin will throw open the gates of heaven and unclog the blessings.

Instead of yielding, we run from counselor to counselor, from pastor to pastor, from prophet to prophet - trying to find help to cope with despair, emptiness, and restlessness.

Yet, it is all in vain because sin and lust have not yet been plucked out. Sin is the root of all our problems. Peace comes only when we surrender and forsake all lust and secret sin.

No - God will not allow us to drink from stolen waters, then attempt to drink at His holy fountain. Not only will our secret sin find us out, it will deny us God's best and bring on a flood of despair, doubt, and fear.

Do not blame God for not answering your prayers if you're not listening to His call to obedience.

You will end up blaspheming God and accusing Him of negligence, while all along you are the culprit.

❖

Un-forgiveness

CHRIST WILL NOT deal with anyone with a wrathful and unforgiving spirit. We are commanded to *"lay aside all malice, envy, and evil speaking, and as newborn babes, desire the sincere milk of the Word" (1 Peter 2:1, 2).*

Christ will not even communicate with a wrangling, jangling, unforgiving person.

God's law of prayer is clear on this matter, *"Lift up pure hands without wrath or doubting" 1 Timothy 2:8.*

By not forgiving the sins committed against us, we make it impossible for God to forgive and bless us. He instructed us to pray, *"Forgive us, as we forgive others." In the Lord's Prayer*

Is there a grudge smoldering in your heart against another? Don't look upon it as something you have a right to indulge in. God takes such things very seriously.

All the wrangling and disputing among Christian brothers and sisters must grieve His heart more than all the sins of the ungodly.

No wonder our prayers are hindered - we have become so obsessed with our own hurt feelings and so concerned about our mistreatment from others.

There is also a malignant mistrust rising up in religious circles. Jealousies, charitableness, bitterness, competition, gossip - and a spirit of revenge, all in God's name.

We should not wonder if God shuts the very gates of heaven on us, until we learn to love and forgive.

Yes, even those who have hurt us the most. Get this

Jonah off your ship and the storm will settle.

❖

Do not prescribe how God Should Answer

IT'S OKAY to keep asking but we should be flexible enough to allow God to answer us however He wants. He is a good Father, better than our earthly parents.

The only person we lay down terms to is the one we don't trust. Those we trust we leave to themselves to do what is right.

Dictating how God should answer us all boils down to our lack of trust in Him.

The believing soul, after he has unburdened his heart in prayer to the Lord, resigns himself to the faithfulness, goodness, and wisdom of God.

The true believer will leave the shaping of the answer to God's mercy. Whatever way God chooses to answer; the believer will welcome it.

David prayed diligently for his household, and then committed all to God's covenant - *"Though my house be not so with God, yet He hath made with me a covenant" (2 Samuel 23:5).*

Those who prescribe to God how and when to answer actually limit the Holy One of Israel.

Since God will not bring the answer in the front door, they are not aware of His coming in the back. They trust only in conclusions and not promises.

But God will not be bound up to time, manner, or means of answering. He will forever do exceedingly, abundantly more than we ask or think of asking.

He will answer with health, or grace that is better than health.

He will send love, or something beyond it. He will deliver or do something even greater.

He desires that we simply leave our requests lodged in His powerful arms, cast all our care upon Him, and go forth with peace and serenity to wait His relief.

How tragic to have so great a God and confident but so little faith in Him.

Chapter 8

CONCLUSION

The Necessity of Prayer

WE CAN BE ANGRY at God for not giving us what we ask for when we're asking for a benz, a new house or for our favorite team to win the big game.

But it gets real when our health, or the health of someone we love, begins to fail, or when we've been looking for employment for months and can't find any job.

These are the moments when God's answers are hard to accept; extremely hard that we reject His answer of no, to the point that we can even sometimes turn away from our faith. And it's so wrong.

In all circumstance, unfavorable answers, keep praying, our prayers should be reminders of our trust in God and His wisdom, of our belief that nothing is happening that He is not aware of, or even allowing.

Trusting God is an admission of our limited perspective. God is good, and He is the giver of good gifts.

Trusting Him through His answers that don't make us feel great provides us an opportunity to show that we can love and trust Him despite the hurt from painful circumstances we go through like all the men of God in the bible.

If God takes long to answer, keep reminding yourself of the good He has done for you. David, said

"This is my infirmity, but I will remember the years of the right hand of the Most High, I will remember the works of the Lord, surely I will remember Thy wonders of old." (Psalm 77:10,11).

Trust God, He is faithful. You can be rest assured that when the answer comes, it will come in a way and in a time, it will be most enjoyed.

If what you prayed for is worth praying for, then surely, it is worth the wait.

Be patient in waiting.

We serve an all-powerful God: He is never concerned about the power of His enemies, but rather the impatience of His own people - us.

He is bigger than all your enemies combined, bigger than all the problems of this world combined.

God loves you, trust Him. He wants you to rely and depend on Him like little children on their parents.

Hold onto His promises, remind Him of what He has promised you, don't forget to also remind the devil of what God has promised you.

Have hope, do not give up, do not be discouraged, at the right time He shall come through for you.

Stay away from sin, God will not permit a liar or sinner to enter His Kingdom or to receive from Him.

Have faith, there are times I go ahead of time and thank God for giving me things am praying for now. Sometimes the things I am praying for, are for next months, next year, 10 years to come, but still I say, thank you for giving me these at that time of the future.

Keep this in mind, it is us who stand to lose if we do not get back to watching and praying.

We become cold, sensuous, and playful, so carnal, too sensitive, too emotional, and make the worst mistakes, when we avoid the secret closet of prayer.

What a sad awakening there will be for those who carelessly harbor secret grudges against the Lord for not answering their prayers, when all along they have been is lazy to pray.

To this point, we have not been effectual and fervent yet..

We have not shut ourselves in with Him. We are living sinful lives and yet we expect Him to give us what we want? Really brethren?

Just because He has not given it to us, we have turned to be doubtful, unbelieving, how will this help us in getting what we want?

We have been materialistic, seeking after the things of this world, forgetting that we have to seek first His Kingdom and His Righteousness; we ask of Him things for wrong reasons and yet we wonder why He is not giving us those?

Can you identify with Job? You cry out to God in your affliction and you see nothing change. It seems like He's just standing there watching you writhe. It feels cruel.

But this is not a fact. What is true is that God is doing far more than we know.

For Job, he did not know that he was putting Satan to shame by trusting in God despite his desolate confusion.

He did not know that his experience would encourage millions of people into the future. And like Job, we do not know what mind-blowing designs God has in store for what may feel unbearable and appear cruel today.

We do not know what testimonies we will have, like the testimonies of Job.

One thing we know is, God was answering Job when it seemed He wasn't, and this might be you right now.

Your suffering may be too much to bear today. But in reality, it is preparing for you *"an eternal weight of glory beyond all comparison" (2 Corinthians 4:17).* Take heart and hold on.

'And after you have suffered a little while, the God of all grace, who has called you to his eternal glory in Christ, will himself restore, confirm, strengthen, and establish you.' (1 Peter 5:10)

Sometimes the answer is "no" or He chooses to answer differently that what we prayed for simply because God Sees the bigger picture of our lives.

If God doesn't give us what we are asking for, we have to remember that He has a good plan and a purpose for everything in our lives and He only wants the very best for us.

He is looking at everything from an eternal perspective. Our time on earth is meant to prepare us for eternity. God cares about our physical needs, but

He is infinitely more concerned about our spiritual needs and growth.

This is where knowing God's character and knowing His promises makes a huge difference. When we have faith and trust in Him, then we can rest knowing that He hears our prayers, sees our needs and He is faithful to answer according to His will, which is always the best.

Sometimes, the answer is wait. There is value in waiting. There are many lessons to be taught in our periods of waiting. There are so many examples in the bible, of those who had to wait, sometimes for a very long period of time before they saw God's promises fulfilled and their prayers answered. God is never late or early. He is always right on time. Trust Him, in your waiting.

Of course, it is easy to grow weary, discouraged, frustrated and impatient in our times of waiting. But at the end, we have to trust God a little more and take Him at His Word.

There are many things that we will never know, or understand, this side of heaven, things like, why some people are healed and others aren't, why some people are spared from tragedies and others aren't, but we need to know that when our prayers aren't answered, it doesn't mean it's because we are necessarily doing something wrong, sometimes we can be doing everything right, remember, when we are living a life that is pleasing to God, we are more of a target for the enemy.

We must remember that we live in a fallen world and there is evil in this world. God created this world to be perfect, but sin entered in.

God does not cause evil, God does not cause anyone to sin or do bad things, yet God gets blamed for a lot of things that are not His doing. And it's so unfair to Him.

God made a way for us through Jesus, and God does promise to work all things together for good for those who love Him. He will redeem what the enemy has meant for our harm.

We know that there will be suffering in this world, and that we will share in the suffering of Christ, so we should not believe those who misinterpret scripture to say if we have enough faith, then we will never be sick, or that if we are sick, it's because there is sin in our lives, or we have done something wrong, or its punishment.

Do not believe everything outside the Word of God, things like the above are not from God.

The bible is full of examples of people that followed God and were beloved by Him yet faced every form of adversity here on earth.

Sometimes God allows things to happen to us for our own good.

We can pray, asking in faith and believing with all of our hearts that God can and will heal us, but at times, He doesn't choose to heal in this life because He has a greater plan and purpose for our lives through that illness or infirmity.

What the enemy has meant for our harm and destroy us; what the enemy hoped would be a stumbling block to our faith, God will turn around and redeem and use for our good and His glory.

If we do not spend time learning God's word and obeying what we learned, we should not expect God to answer our prayers. King Solomon says in the book of proverbs, that prayers made from a hardened heart are an abomination to God.

"If one turns away his ear from hearing the law, even his prayer is an abomination" (Proverbs 28:9)

God speaks to us through His Word. If we disobey what He teaches, He will not answer our prayers.

"Now we know that God hears not sinners: but if any man be a worshipper of God, and does His will, him He hears (John 9:31)

"The eyes of the lord are on the righteous, and His ears are attentive to their cry;" (Psalm 34:15)

"The Lord is far from the wicked, but He hears the prayer of the righteous." (Proverbs 15:29)

"If I had cherished sin in my heart, the Lord would not have listened" (Psalm 66:18)

"He fulfills the desires of those who fear Him; He hears their cry and saves them". (Psalm 145:19)

No matter what the issues is God always wants people to do the right thing and to make choices that are in alignment with His will and His commandments, but God gave us free will and God will never force someone to make the correct choices, but they will have to live with the consequences of their choices and their choices and actions might also affect others.

When we are affected by the negative choices of others, a believer can be rest assured that God will redeem which the enemy meant for harm in our lives.

He will do as He promises in *Romans 8:28* to work all things together for good for those who believe.

God does miracles in lives that are yielded to Him. Persistent prayer changes things....

---------------------- Pray! --------------------------

-------------------And do not give up! ------------------

Made in the USA
Middletown, DE
17 March 2019